Indelible Ink

Indelible Ink

Adventures of a Baby Boomer

Timothy J. Fields

illustrated by
N.C. Hall

Fields Publishing
Nashville, Tennessee

Printed in the United States of America

Library of Congress Card Number: 2002104197

ISBN:1-57843-015-1 (softback book)
ISBN:1-57843-016-X (hardback book)

Cover Design by Dru Drolsum
Tammy Drolsum, manuscript editor

Published by

FIELDS
PUBLISHING

Fields Publishing Inc.
917 Harpeth Valley Place • Nashville, Tennessee 37221
615-662-1344
e-mail: tfields@fieldspublishing.com

Contents

Foreword

I am among the first of the baby boomers, those persons born between 1946 and 1964. We are so called because of the post World War II boom in births. I have never kept a written diary. However, certain life events have been imprinted in my mind as though they were written in indelible ink.

I wrote the entries in this book as I remember them. Some of the facts may have been altered slightly by time and failing memory. Some of these memories seem insignificant and why they remain with me I'll leave to the psychiatrists and psychologists.

These events are permanent imprints on the pages of my life. I am powerless to erase them. We are all products of our past, and we are sometimes forever altered by both positive and negative events.

This book is a collection of some of those indelible ink moments that have become a part of who I am—moments such as my "ride" on a bucking bronco frozen in midair by a Colorado taxidermist on one of only three vacations my family ever took together.

Some of the events I look forward to revisiting. Other memories of unhappy or painful events, I would like to blot out. Most of my lasting memories involve other people. Looking back on my life I am convinced that the investments that yield the highest returns are the investments we make in the lives of others. All of us have the capacity to receive and to dispense indelible ink memories.

Sometimes a simple comment from a parent to a child or from a teacher to a pupil can have a profound effect on someone's life. Even a smile, a frown, a wink or a raised eyebrow can dispense indelible ink. A congratulatory pat on the back or a punitive slap on the cheek can remain in a person's psyche for life.

Not only what happens to us in life but how we cope with those events determines who we become. My most memorable moments have been strongly influenced by family, friends, and most of all, by faith in God. Whenever my family recalls the good moments in life and now even laughs about the bad times, it helps us to relish the mountaintop experiences and to learn from and endure the troublesome days.

I hope these life stories will help you to recall, reassess and relish the indelible ink moments written on the pages of your own life.

—Tim Fields, May 2003

Acknowledgements

Writing a book was a dream that began when I was a teenager in Salina, Kansas. Forty years later my experiences are enough to fill these pages and more.

I owe the fulfillment of this dream to my family, friends, teachers, co-workers and others who left their indelible ink on my life.

Thanks go to my oldest daughter Tammy Drolsum, who edited my entries; to my son-in-law Dru Drolsum, who designed the book cover and made other valuable contributions; to Leonard Hill and my wife Linda Fields who helped proofread the book, and to Nancy Hall, whose illustrations add visual life to the stories.

Special thanks go to the principle players in this book—my parents Alfred and Lucille Fields, who both died several years ago; my four brothers Steve, Bill, Phil and Dan; my wife Linda; my sister-in-law Judy who introduced Linda to me; and to my daughters Tammy, Christy and Becky who continually urged me to write down these stories that I told them many times over the years. I also extend thanks to my newest son-in-law Stefan Gore, who lost his father at an untimely age but who has "adopted" me and has become my encourager.

Finally, thanks to my granddaughters Aden and Lindy, who with their inexhaustible energy and their sweet actions and indelible words have inspired and energized me to write and publish this book. —Tim Fields

Entry 1

Teddy Bear's Tongue

1948—Wichita, Kansas

On my second birthday my parents gave me a fuzzy brown teddy bear. He was the color of cinnamon. I loved Teddy. I took him everywhere I went. I took my bear on trips and slept with him every night for several years. One of my favorite pictures in my family album is of me with my teddy bear taken March 21, 1948—the day he came to live with me.

The bear had movable arms and legs and a head that was secured to a round cardboard disk in his body that allowed him to turn his head completely around. My teddy bear's eyes were made of shiny black leather buttons, and his nostrils were delicately sewn in dark brown thread. His little smile was embroidered with bright red thread.

However, in spite of his handsome appearance, my teddy bear had a bad habit. He had a pink tongue that stuck out of his mouth. My mother told me after I was older that she was attracted to the bear in the store because of its "cute little tongue."

That "cute little tongue" was soon to be the source of problems for teddy bear and me. Not long after my birthday, my mother found a piece of pink felt on the floor near the sewing box and didn't know what it was until she realized my teddy bear had lost its tongue.

"Timmy," my mother exclaimed, "look—your teddy bear lost its

10

little pink tongue, and I found it. I'll sew it back on, and he'll be cute as ever."

A few weeks later my mother discovered the tongue had fallen off again. It was lying beside the sewing box again. "Timmy, are you pulling on your teddy bear's tongue?" my mother asked. I didn't answer. "You have to be careful not to be rough with your bear," she said.

A few weeks afterward, my mother found me beside her sewing box with scissors in hand. The bear was on my lap, but his little limp tongue was lying beside me on the floor. "Timmy, what have you done? Did you cut off your teddy bear's tongue?"

"Yes," I replied sheepishly, "I don't like his tongue."

"But Timmy, that little tongue is so cute. Why don't you like it?" my mother asked.

"Mother, you told me it's not nice to stick your tongue out at people, and I don't like my bear sticking its tongue out at me," I explained. "It's bad manners, and it makes me feel bad. I'm trying to make him behave."

"Oh Timmy, now I understand. Have you been cutting your bear's tongue off each time I sew it on?" my mother asked.

"Yes," I softly replied.

"Well Timmy, this is your bear, and I think you're right. It's not polite for people or bears to stick their tongues out at others," my mother replied. "We'll just leave the tongue off."

Then my mother knelt down and looked at me for a long time. "I love you, Timmy," she said softly as she patted me on the top of my head and then patted my bear on the top of his head. She smiled and placed the scissors back in the sewing box.

Throughout their lives my parents used every opportunity to teach my brothers and me lessons for right living. Instead of reprimanding me for cutting off my teddy bear's tongue, my mother's loving and wise response reinforced my desire to continue to follow her guidance. My mother was perceptive enough to realize I was following her teachings on good manners and that I was attempting to teach them to my furry playmate.

More than half a century later my teddy bear sits on a beam high atop my den keeping watch over my grandchildren whenever they

come to play. Like his owner, Teddy's a little worse for wear. His fur is thin in places; the black leather on his beady eyes is worn and scratchy; and his head sags a little.

Often as I enter the front door to my home, I glance up at Teddy on his high perch where he can look out the tall windows and watch the sun rise each morning. He looks back at me with his little threadbare smile. He sits in the bed of my old orange and white Structo toy grain truck and seems content with himself. I am proud to say Teddy learned his lesson early in life. He never again stuck his tongue out at me or at anyone else—and neither did I.

Entry 2

Bossy The Cow

1949—Jetmore, Kansas

One of my earliest memories as a child was when I was nearly three years old. My father was pastor of a small Baptist church in Jetmore, Kansas, a tiny farming community.

Like most pastors of small rural churches in the late 1940s, my father's salary was meager. Church members often brought fruits, vegetables and other produce from their farms to help the pastor and his family.

Our parsonage was a small white-frame bungalow heated with a coal-fired furnace and located on the town's main street a few doors down from the church. My parents kept a milk cow in a pasture on the edge of town.

One of the church families had loaned the big brown Jersey cow to my parents to provide fresh milk for our family. With the loan of Bossy came free use of a small cow shed and some pasture land.

One morning my father invited me to go with him to meet Bossy the cow and to help him with the milking. I had never seen Bossy, and I was excited and a little nervous about milking the cow.

After a brief ride, we arrived at the pasture. Bossy's shed was at the foot of a steep grassy hill. As we started down the hill to get my first glimpse of Bossy, my father took my hand in his and said, "Timmy, we need to walk slowly down this steep hill. There are a lot of rocks, and I don't want you to fall down and get hurt."

At that moment I caught sight of Bossy the cow. She was enormous. Bossy had a big leather collar, and the bell around her neck was clanging as she moved her head. She was chewing a large mouthful of grass, and she looked directly at me as we started down the hill.

"Bossy, Bossy!" I squealed as I pulled away from father's hand and began running down the hill.

"Timmy, slow down!" my father shouted. It was too late. Before I could heed my father's urgent warning, my legs were flailing in front of me like a Kansas windmill. I tried to slow down, but instead my legs pounded faster and faster. I plunged headfirst and somersaulted down the hill. As I came to rest only a few feet from the startled hulk of a cow, I felt a stabbing pain in the palm of my left hand. I had fallen on the base of a broken milk bottle.

I looked up, and Bossy was staring back at me with her big brown bulging eyes and long eyelashes. Before I could utter a cry, my father scooped me up and immediately placed my little hand in his. He pressed his big thumb into the wound in the palm of my hand, and the pain vanished. My father turned and dashed back up the hill holding me in his strong arms.

"Where are we going, Daddy?" I asked. "I want to see Bossy the cow."

"We've got to take you to the hospital to make sure you are OK," my father replied.

"But I'm alright, I'm not hurt. I want to see Bossy the cow," I pleaded.

"We'll come back and see Bossy later," my father said as he sat me on his lap behind the big steering wheel of the car.

My father steered and shifted the car with his right hand while he continued to hold my hand in his left hand. His thumb was still firmly pressed into the palm of my hand.

We sped away, and within a few minutes we were at the small hospital where my father had gone many times to visit church members when they were sick.

My father gently carried me inside. "Hello, Reverend Fields. Who is that with you?" an older lady in a white dress and funny white hat asked.

"It's my son Timothy, and he's been hurt. I think he'll need some stitches," my father firmly replied.

"Bring Timmy in here and I'll get the doctor," the nice lady said.

My father sat down on a padded table covered with a clean white sheet and clutched me in his arms still holding my hand in his own.

The doctor appeared almost instantly. I remember he was wearing a long white coat and had a tube with a silver metal circle hanging around his neck.

"Timmy, I understand you've been hurt. Let me take a look at your hand," the doctor said.

"No, I'm not hurt," I replied. "I just fell down a hill when I went to see Bossy our cow."

My father extended my little hand to the doctor, and as he did he released his thumb. Immediately a gaping wound appeared in the palm of my hand. Blood instantly flowed down my wrist and onto my leg and made large red splotches on the white sheet. The sharp pain I felt when I landed on the broken glass at the feet of Bossy the cow returned, and I started to cry.

"It's OK, Timmy, we'll fix you up good as new," the doctor assured. After cleaning the wound and giving me a shot, the doctor sewed my palm back together with eight stitches and wrapped a bandage around my hand.

"There, we're all done Timmy," the doctor said.

"Thank you, Dr. Wilson," my father said as he picked me up in his comforting arms and carried me outside to the car.

He sat me on his lap again and let me pretend to drive the car back to the parsonage.

More than fifty years later the scar from this injury is still indelibly etched in the palm of my hand. I can count the holes where the country doctor closed my wound with his needle and thread.

I have thought about this incident many times over the years. As I grew older and my parents taught me about God's provisions for my life, I viewed my earthly father's actions that day as an example of God's care for his children.

When I was injured and in pain my father held my hand in his. The pressure of his big thumb on my small injured palm kept me from fully realizing I had been hurt. Not until he released the pressure of his thumb did I know how much I needed his loving care. Instead of helping to milk a big brown cow named Bossy, I experienced the love of a wise and caring father.

My brother Stephen once asked my father why Catholic priests were called "Father."

"Don't call any man your father, not even me," he instructed. "God is your only true father. I'm just your Dad."

My dad's care for me that day reminds me that God is ever present in the lives of those who call upon Him and invite Him into their lives. He does not promise us a life free of pain, heartache or injury. However, God promises His constant presence and stands ready to comfort us when we inevitably fall headlong. Our Heavenly Father holds each of us in His strong arms, and with His thumb on the pulsebeat of our life, He gives us the strength to overcome our doubts, temptations and adversities.

Entry 3

Mighty Mouse

1951—Wichita, Kansas

When I was five years old my family lived in Wichita, Kansas. My mother was a wonderful cook, and I was always ready whenever she called my brothers and me to a meal. One afternoon while my older brother Steve was at Gardiner Elementary School, where he was in first grade, I found one of his *Mighty Mouse* comic books. It showed pictures of this super mouse saving children from harm and battling evil wherever he went.

I showed my mother the comic book and asked her to read it to me. When she was finished, I said, "Mom, can I play like I'm Mighty Mouse and save people?"

"Sure," she replied. "Come here Timmy. I'll make you a costume." My mom found an old red pajama top and a blue towel for a cape that she secured around my shoulders with a safety pin. She took one of my father's old ties and tied it around my waist for a belt.

I played most of the morning, running around the house and singing at the top of my voice: "Here I come to save the day. Mighty Mouse is on his way." I was familiar with the song because I had heard it on the radio and had seen Mighty Mouse in cartoons at the movie theater where Steve and I often went on Saturday mornings for 15 cents each.

For several hours I pretended I was saving my little brother Billy, who was two years old. I would climb up on the couch and then jump down, run past him and grab him in my arms, saving him from dangerous wild animals, speeding cars and hoodlums who were chasing him.

By the time my brother Steve came home from school, I was hungry and thirsty from my lifesaving adventures. My mother was preparing a delicious supper of stewed chicken and homemade noodles, and I begged for something to eat and drink. Her samplings of raw noodle dough cut into small strips were tasty and usually appeased me, but I had spied a large round tub of vanilla ice cream when my mother opened the small freezer door to pour me a drink of ice water.

"Oh Mom, can I have some ice cream? I'm so hungry. Please Mom!" I pleaded.

"No, Timmy, you can't have any ice cream until after dinner. Your father will be home pretty soon, and after your meal you can have some ice cream."

"No," I pouted as I placed my arms across my chest and proclaimed, "I'm Mighty Mouse and I've been saving people all day and I want some ice cream now!"

"Timmy, don't ask me again or I'll send you to your room. No ice cream until dinner—even for Mighty Mouse," my mother replied firmly.

I don't know what came over me at that moment, but I ran into my bedroom, put on my Mighty Mouse cape and ran back into the dining room where my mother was setting the table for dinner.

"Mom, if you don't give me some ice cream right now, I am going to really become Mighty Mouse and smash through the living room window and fly away and never come back," I said forcefully.

"Timmy, I told you 'no.' Now go to your room and stay there until supper time."

"You'll be sorry, Mom," I said as I put my arms straight out in front of me and took careful aim at the picture window in the living room at the front of the house.

"Mighty Mouse" took off, running at full speed. My intention was to grab the sides of the window with my outstretched hands and come to a dead stop. Instead of grabbing the frame around the window, which was wider than my outstretched hands, I crashed through the window with a deafening shatter. Shards of glass filled the air around me as I came to a stop with my hands and upper body hanging out the window. I didn't utter a word. I was in a state of shock.

My mother raced to the window and gently pulled me back into the room. She examined me from head to toe and exclaimed, "Timmy, what on earth has come over you? You're lucky you didn't kill yourself!" By the grace of God I emerged from my flight with only a few small cuts and scrapes on my hands and arms. My mom took me to the bathroom, removed my cape and cleaned and bandaged my wounds.

"Dad is going to whip the tar out of you when he gets home, Timmy," Steve warned. "You'll never get another allowance as long as you live," he assured.

Mother sent me to my bedroom and then taped a large piece of cardboard over the broken window. A little while after my father arrived home, I heard his loud voice as he discussed my "mishap" with my mother. I was prepared for the worst as my mother came into the room and told me supper was ready. As I sat down at the table, my father never said a word. He simply glanced across the room at the broken window, looked down at my bandaged hands and then looked me straight in the eye. I could tell he was extremely disappointed in my actions. I think my mother had somehow calmed him down. His facial expression was worse than the spanking I expected from him.

Our family enjoyed an unusually quiet but delicious meal of chicken, homemade noodles and broth, cottage cheese, green beans and milk.

At the close of the meal, my mother dipped up large bowls of ice cream for everyone but me.

Before Mother sat down again she came up behind me and placed her hands on my shoulders and then kissed me on the cheek. "If Mighty Mouse will learn that he, too, has to follow the rules, then he can have his ice cream tomorrow after his lunch," my mother announced.

I wanted to protest, but the stern look in my father's eyes told me that Mighty Mouse had gotten off easy and that he better not complain. "OK, Mom, I think he's learned his lesson," I said sheepishly.

The next day I was a good helper. I dried the breakfast dishes, helped Mother clean house and was especially kind to my little brother Billy. After a lunch of roast beef sandwiches and sweet pickles, my mother went to the freezer and dipped up an unusually large bowl of vanilla ice cream and placed it on the table before me. It was the best bowl of ice cream Mighty Mouse had ever eaten.

Entry 4

Best Christmas Ever

1953—Wichita, Kansas

Christmas was fast approaching and my mother had warned my brothers and me that we might not find many presents under the tree this year. The warning came after my two younger brothers and I had requested stick horses for Christmas.

My father was the pastor of a small Baptist church in Wichita, Kansas, at the time, but the church could not pay him a large enough salary to support a family. He had begun selling aluminum cookware door-to-door to supplement our income. I knew things were tight because my grandparents on my mother's side came to visit quite often and brought glass jars of fruits, vegetables and jellies they had canned from harvesting their large home garden in the spare lots behind and beside their home.

My father would bring home delicious apple, peach and cherry pies from his mother, who worked as a pastry cook in a small restaurant on Douglas Avenue in Wichita.

From the vast array of food at dinnertime we seemed to be doing quite well. However, several times I overheard my parents discussing finances. They said they didn't know how they were going to pay the house payment and the utility bills. My oldest brother Steve was 11 years old, I was 7 and brothers Bill and Phil were 6 and 4 respectively.

Steve was doing odd jobs to earn money to help our family. Phil, Bill and I spent much of our free time after school and on Saturdays playing cowboys with other boys on the 2200 block of South Victoria Street.

We all had guns and holsters, but the Fields boys were the only ones on the block who did not have stick horses to ride. We had to pretend. The other boys often made fun of us because we didn't have horses.

"We have horses. They are just invisible," we told the other boys. They were not convinced. Most of the neighbor boys' horses were alike. The horses' heads were cut in silhouette form from flat pieces of wood and painted, usually with a white background. The horses' eyes, nose and mouth were painted in black.

Most had pieces of thin rope nailed to the head for the reins and an unpainted broomstick to straddle when "riding" the horse.

The boy that teased us the most had an official Roy Rogers "Trigger" horse that was painted pale yellow with black features and black reins. It was especially striking.

Although we were disappointed that we wouldn't get stick horses for Christmas, it didn't keep us from chasing outlaws on our pretend horses that could change colors daily at our whim. One day I could ride a black stallion and the next an Appaloosa. We were only limited by what kind of horse we could conjure up and describe to our playmates. Our identities could change as well. We chose who would be the robbers or outlaws and who would play the roles of our cowboy heroes Gene Autry, Hopalong Cassidy, Roy Rogers and The Lone Ranger. The most coveted character to role play was Tonto, the Lone Ranger's Indian sidekick. Tonto was strong, brave, loyal and mysterious.

A few days before Christmas we returned home from an adventure-filled afternoon of playing cowboys and Indians on our invisible horses. As we ran into the house and headed straight for the bathroom, we surprised our mother, who was standing in the bathtub with an old apron around her waist, a paintbrush in one hand and a small can of red paint in the other. Hanging from a bare shower curtain rod were three broomsticks glistening with bright red paint. The fumes from the fresh paint filled the bathroom in spite of the partially opened bathroom window.

"Oh, you boys surprised me," she said. "I didn't expect you home so soon. Wash up and we'll have supper in a few minutes," she said with a smile.

"Why in the world are you painting those red sticks, Mom?" I asked.

"What are you going to do with those smelly things?" Bill queried.

"Well, boys, they're for a little project I'm working on," she replied cheerily. "Don't touch the broomsticks—the paint is still wet. You'll find out later what they are for," she said with a gleam in her eyes.

We were hungry and soon forgot about the sticks, which were gone by the time we were ready for our Saturday evening baths in preparation for church attendance on Sunday.

The days flew by, and Christmas Eve arrived. My father took us to purchase our tree from the Boy Scouts Christmas tree lot. He loved to bargain and informed the boys he was an Eagle Scout (the highest rank in scouting) and asked if that qualified him for a discount. They told my father he could have the tree for 50 cents since it was so close to Christmas and they would have to discard it if it hadn't sold by the end of the day.

My father seemed pleased with his purchase, and he brought the tree home for us to decorate. We trimmed the tree with popcorn we strung with needle and thread and with ornaments made out of tinfoil and construction paper. We had a string of lights and some used metallic icicles from the previous Christmas. We hung a small homemade star on top of the tree to symbolize the star that guided the shepherds to baby Jesus on that first Christmas in Bethlehem. We positioned a white bulb from the string of lights so it illuminated the star.

Christmas morning dawned bright and sunny. We knew not to expect much, but all four of us boys were awake in our beds and on the count of "One, two, three, go!" we all clamored out of bed and ran for the tree in the living room.

Under the tree were numerous presents wrapped in *Wichita Eagle* newspaper comic pages. It was a colorful array. Leaned against a corner by the tree were three long packages almost as tall as we boys. We ran to my parents' bedroom to awaken them and then we all returned to the living room to unwrap our presents. Mom seemed excited as each of us opened packages from our grandparents that contained pajamas, socks and oranges wrapped in colored tissue paper.

At last, all the presents had been opened except for the three tall ones in the corner. Mom asked Steve to distribute the presents to Bill, Phil and me. Steve had already opened his presents from my parents. He received a green wool sweater with a moose head embroidered in white yarn and a Boy Scout pocket knife.

Now it was time for each of us to open our last present. As we tore into the newspaper comic wrapping we all shouted with glee.

We lined up in order of age and mounted the most beautiful stick horses we had ever seen.

My mother had taken men's slacks that my father had outgrown when he gained weight and made three-dimensional horses' heads that she had stuffed with scraps of material. Billy's horse and mine were fine gray steeds fashioned from a blue-gray pair of tweed pants. Phil's horse was smaller and was chocolate brown. The material had come from an old set of window drapes.

Mother had meticulously fashioned anatomically accurate heads. She was familiar with how a real horse should look. As a farm girl she had ridden horses and was almost killed one time when she and her sisters slid off a horse while riding it bareback up a steep, muddy bank.

Mother carefully fashioned the eyes, nose and mouth on each of our stick horses with embroidery thread. The mane on each horse was made from beautiful soft yarn that lay in tight curls against each horse's head and neck.

The ears were perky three-dimensional creations that pointed upward, giving our steeds an alert and poised appearance.

My mother had fashioned intricate bridles and reins out of women's old plastic belts fastened together at all the joints with bright shiny gold brads.

The horses' heads were attached at the neck to bright shiny red broomsticks by upholstery tacks. They were the same broomsticks that had been hanging in our bathroom to dry only a few days earlier.

We hugged and kissed our mother and father and spent hours admiring and riding our new horses throughout the house.

As we met the neighbor boys later that Christmas morning, they were in total awe of our new stick horses that appeared more real than any they had ever seen before. We proudly rode our steeds for several years and never once made fun of the flat dime-store horses our friends continued to ride.

With lots of work, abundant love and a little money, my parents had given us the best Christmas ever.

Entry 5

Monkey Socks

1960–1975—Wichita, Kansas; Salina, Kansas

Many of our friends admired the stick horses our mother made for us for our best Christmas ever. Her next toy animal creation was a monkey fashioned from mens' gray or brown herringbone work socks with red heels. The red heels formed the mouth and hindquarters of the monkey. She planned to make her first monkey for my brother Dan, who had requested one for his sixth birthday. Dan recalls coming home from kindergarten to find a curious sight on the family dining room table.

Scattered across the table was a wide assortment of monkey parts—ears, tails, arms, legs, eyes and two heads. He knew his monkey wouldn't have two heads, so he was puzzled by the overabundance of monkey pieces and parts.

As my mother entered the room from the kitchen Dan asked her, "Mom why are there two monkey heads and so many arms, legs and other parts?"

"Well, Danny, your cousin Karen is in the hospital and she is

27

very sick. I decided to make her a monkey, too. I need to make her monkey first, and I may not finish your monkey until after your birthday. I hope you will understand."

What my mother did not tell Dan was that Karen's kidneys were failing and she was not expected to live much longer.

Fortunately, with her new monkey at her bedside decked out in a little pink doll dress and hat, Karen's health slowly improved and the crisis passed. Dan's monkey arrived on his birthday after all, and he named him "Bobo."

My mother made many sock monkeys and other handcrafted creations over the years, including monkeys and dolls for her grandchildren. Most of those monkeys have survived years of love and handling by their owners and are treasured possessions, including Bobo, who is now more than 40 years old.

Although she was a college-educated woman, my mother never worked outside the home after my oldest brother Steve was born. As a result, our family income was limited. However, she was always available to dispense her faith in God, along with her love, wisdom and homemaking skills such as cooking, sewing and ironing, to her five sons and to others. The stuffed animals my mother created with inexpensive materials became invaluable because of the indelible imprints of her love and care.

During a recent visit to my brother Phil's home, my niece and nephew retrieved the monkeys my mother—their grandmother—had made years ago. Both monkeys showed wear from years of handling and were individually tailored for their owners. My nephew's monkey had overalls and a jacket. My niece's monkey wore a petite dress and sunbonnet.

With monkeys in hand, the memories of their grandmother poured from their lips like honey onto a freshly baked biscuit. My mother's love and wisdom expressed through simple materials such as work socks, cotton stuffing and thread had become priceless works of art providing comfort and love long after her death.

Entry 6

Mary Virginia's Dishes

1953—Wichita, Kansas

I was in first grade at Gardiner Elementary in Wichita, Kansas. We lived on Victoria Street in a gray and white wooden siding house with windows that looked like little doghouses protruding from the front of the roof.

At that time I had only three brothers. My brothers and I used to tease that if my mother were to give birth to a girl we would throw her in the trash can. That's before any of us realized that girls are special and marvelous creatures.

Maybe our unenthusiastic attitude toward girls stemmed from our experience with Mary Virginia, an unkempt, unruly, bossy 8-year-old girl who lived next door. Mary Virginia and her brother Kenny ran wild in the neighborhood, and their parents fought frequently.

One day I heard Kenny's mother screaming at him as he climbed out the first-floor bedroom window carrying a half-full quart-sized liquor bottle. He was stark naked, and he streaked down the middle of the street waving the bottle back and forth as his mother pursued him, screaming obscenities.

We never knew from day to day what drama might unfold next door. Mary Virginia and Kenny often were left at home alone, and they always seemed to be playing in our yard. Like many girls her age, Mary Virginia was experiencing a growth spurt and was a head taller than any of my brothers or me. She used to push, shove and sass us as well as the other kids in our neighborhood.

One windy spring day Mary Virginia pranced proudly out of her house carrying a cardboard box filled with petite plastic dishes, cups and saucers. She approached my brothers and me and informed us that we were all going to play house with her.

"No, we are not going to play house with you," my kindergarten-age brother Billy pronounced. "We don't play with sissy stuff," he asserted as he crossed his arms against his chest.

While we boys played cowboys and Indians, Mary Virginia methodically laid out each of her blue and white plastic dishes, cups, saucers and assorted teapots and sugar bowls in a long line on the edge of our driveway. The dishes were imprinted with dainty blue daisies around the edges.

When she had arranged all of the dishes to her satisfaction, Mary Virginia ran toward us and climbed the three steps up to our small concrete front porch where Billy and I were standing. "You boys get down here right now," Mary Virginia ordered. "We are going to play house."

"I told you we are not going to play house," Billy answered defiantly.

"Alright then, you stupid boy," Mary Virginia screamed back as she plunged both hands into Billy's chest and knocked him backwards off the porch. Billy's head hit the sidewalk below with a loud thump like a ripe watermelon. Mary Virginia laughed and ran past Billy, who was lying flat on his back nearly unconscious. I raced down the steps to help my brother. After Billy caught his breath, he began to cry. My Mother appeared at the front door and then rushed out to help Billy.

As I looked up I saw Mary Virginia standing by the long row of dainty dishes with her hands on her hips. "That serves you right, Billy Boy," she yelled sarcastically.

In a fit of rage I rushed toward Mary Virginia. I wanted to punch her eyes out for hurting Billy. I stopped in my tracks in front of Mary Virginia with my hands clenched into tight fists. Mary Virginia returned my glare with a snide smirk. Her little blond head was cocked to one side. I somehow resisted the urge to harm Mary Virginia. I relaxed my hands and turned away from her as I thought of another idea. I proceeded to make my way down our driveway, stomping on every plastic plate, saucer, cup, teapot and sugar bowl in my precisely plotted path, filling the air with loud, brittle crunching sounds. As the Kansas wind began to nudge the pieces of the plastic toy dinner set down the driveway and into the street, Mary Virginia let out a series of long, shrill shrieks.

When I surveyed the damage, I too was stunned. In an instant of anger and frustration I had destroyed Mary Virginia's entire plastic dinner set—not a single piece remained intact.

Mary Virginia wailed as she ran up and down our driveway trying to retrieve the pieces of her plastic dishes that were swirling in the wind. I turned and calmly walked back toward the porch where my mother was sitting with Billy in her lap. During my tirade Mother had gathered Billy up in her arms to examine the bump on the back of his head and to comfort him.

As I approached Billy he looked at me and then at Mary Virginia. He sat straight up in my mother's lap, stopped whimpering and flashed a smile at me that stretched from ear to ear. Billy's look of satisfaction and admiration confirmed that our minds were in sync. Mary Virginia had finally gotten what she deserved.

What happened next took me totally by surprise. My mother gently sat Billy down on the porch and went straight to Mary Virginia. "Honey, I am sorry Timmy broke all of your dishes," she said. "We will buy you some new ones."

I couldn't believe my ears. My mother was now comforting this snot-nosed, mean-spirited little brat. Before I could protest, my mother was standing in front of me not with a look of "Well done, son" but with a frown that wrinkled her brow above her nose.

"Timmy, why did you break all of Mary Virginia's dishes?" She queried. "What you did was wrong!" She grabbed my hand, pulled me to the front porch and bent me over her knee next to my wounded brother. She proceeded to give me a hard paddling on the behind. Along with the stings from the spanking, I had to endure Mary Virginia's self-satisfied grin as she stopped chasing her broken dishes long enough to enjoy the punishment my Mother was administering.

"Timmy, I want you to remember that two wrongs never make a right," my mother said loudly and firmly for all to hear. "Mary Virginia was wrong for pushing your brother off the porch, and she could have killed him, but you are not a judge and jury."

My mother was true to her word, and when Mary Virginia's mother came home, Mother explained to her what had happened and promised to buy Mary Virginia a new set of dishes. "Oh that's OK," Mary Virginia's mother replied rather curtly. "You don't have to do that." Mary Virginia's mother never once inquired about my brother Billy, who emerged from the incident with a large goose egg on the back of his head.

Several days later my mother presented a set of white plastic dishes with dainty little blue daisies imprinted around the edges to a smug Mary Virginia.

Many times throughout the years my parents and my brothers and I recalled this incident and laughed about Mary Virginia's dishes blowing down the street in little pieces. "That was the hardest spanking I ever gave you," my mother told me years later. "I felt badly for a long time for spanking you. Mary Virginia is really the one who deserved a spanking," she admitted.

I have never had hard feelings against my wise and loving mother who spanked me for destroying Mary Virginia's dishes. My mother used spanking sparingly to discipline her sons. In fact, as the years passed I cherished that incident as one of life's most valuable lessons. Two wrongs truly do not make a right.

My mother taught me that taking an eye for an eye only escalates life's problems. Wars often begin with an attempt to right a small wrong, and then continued retaliations can escalate into massive death and destruction. World peace could be well served if mothers and fathers of the world demonstrated this truth to their sons and daughters early in life.

Although my destruction of Mary Virginia's dishes was far less brutal than if I had chosen to push her off our porch backwards in retaliation, it was wrong.

I must admit, at the time I did not regret jumping up and down on those dishes. However, this incident has tempered my reaction to injustices that have taken place in my life. I now know my actions were wrong. I don't know if Mary Virginia ever thought about this event later in life. I hope she realized that bad behavior often carries its own punishment and can tempt others to make bad decisions as well.

My mother, who loved God with all her heart, soul and mind, knew that obeying Jesus' commandment to "Love your neighbor as yourself" (Matthew 19:19) and his admonition to "do good to those who hate you" (Luke 6:27) is far better than extracting a tooth for a tooth or breaking a cocky little girl's dishes in retaliation for a bump on your brother's head!

The Frog Hunters

1953—Wichita, Kansas

The spring season had been especially rainy. My brothers Bill and Phil and I had been watching the tadpoles in the pools of water in an empty field a few blocks from our house. The tadpoles were in various stages of development. Some were tiny hatchlings, and some had legs. Others had emerged from the pools as small frogs. One of our favorite spring pastimes was frog hunting.

One morning after several days of rain we awoke to a sunny Saturday. My brothers and I were prepared. We and several of the neighbor boys had made plans to go frog hunting when the weather cleared. We knew the time was right because each evening the chorus of frogs croaking in the nearby field grew louder. Sometimes it was hard to sleep when the windows were open. The frogs seemed to be calling to us.

We rushed through breakfast and asked our mother if we could go frog hunting. "Yes boys, you can go, but you must promise me that you won't go beyond the barbed wire fence that borders the railroad tracks," she replied.

"Well why not, Mom?" Bill asked. "That's where the biggest frogs are."

"Because the tracks are dangerous, and I don't want you getting hurt around that fence. A train could run over you," my mother warned.

"OK Mom, we won't go beyond the fence," I promised.

My father always bought our green beans, white hominy and peas in gallon cans at a restaurant supply store because they were cheaper in large quantity. The empty cans made fine collection buckets for our frogs. We placed a piece of screen wire over the top of each can and secured the wire with a large rubber band.

My brothers and I met three of our friends and challenged them to a frog hunting contest. The winners would be in two categories—the first for most frogs captured in an hour and the second for the largest frog.

We were eager for the competition to begin, and we headed for the vacant field at a dead run. The field stretched for nearly a city block and paralleled the railroad tracks and the railroad right of way protected by a four-strand barbed wire fence.

The grass was tall, lush and green, and the frogs were plentiful. The frogs bounced into the air as we chased them in all directions. We yelled and laughed gleefully as we filled our vegetable cans with the lively green creatures. Our shoes and clothes were wet and covered with mud as we ran through the soggy field and even pounced on all fours or landed on our bellies in order to capture the elusive amphibians. The more frogs we collected, the more difficult it was to keep one or more from jumping out of the can as we removed the screen wire to deposit the latest catch.

Time was running out, and in spite of the fact that our buckets grew heavier with the squirming frogs, most of them were small. My brothers and I stopped to count our haul. "Thirty-eight total," Phil called out proudly. "I'm sure we have the most."

At that moment Bill yelled, "Look at that big sucker! Quick, let's get him!"

The chase began with my brothers and me in hot pursuit. It was an enormous frog with bulging eyes. The faster we chased him, the faster he hopped. Finally Bill had the frog in his hands, but he tripped as we reached the barbed wire fence and the enormous creature landed on a large rock on the other side of the fence.

"Come on, Timmy, we've got to get that monster," Billy yelled. "He's the biggest frog I've ever seen."

"No, we can't cross the barbed wire fence—I promised," I reminded Bill.

"Come on, Timmy, Mom will never know," he said. "I told you all of the big frogs lived on the other side of the fence. Come on, scaredy cat. If you don't do this, we're going to lose," Bill urged.

I looked at the enormous frog sitting on the rock staring back at me. He seemed to be daring us to pursue him. "OK," I replied, "but after we catch that big one we've got to get back on the other side of the fence."

I carefully placed my foot on the lower strand of barbed wire and stretched the second strand up as high as it would go. "Hurry up and squeeze through there, Bill," I said. Bill shot though like a rocket, but Phil took his time and was careful not to get caught on the sharp wire barbs.

"Hurry up, Timmy, he's going to get away!" Bill yelled. "Get over here!" As I bent down to crawl between the barbs, the big frog jumped from the rock and Bill screamed out, "He's getting away!"

At that instant, Bill relaxed his grip on the barbed wire, and as I attempted to slip through the fence I felt a stabbing pain in my back. The barb dug deep into my skin. I yelled at the top of my voice and dropped my bucket of frogs. The lid jarred loose and frogs jumped in all directions.

"Bill, help me out of here, quick!" I yelped. "My back is bleeding." My shirt was entangled in the fence, and the harder I tried to get free from the wire, the more it dug into my back. We summoned the other team of frog hunters to help tear my shirt and free me from the barb. The security fence indeed had repelled the intrusion of the frog hunting team from the railroad right of way it was designed to protect.

I could feel the warm blood trickle down my back as I grimaced and waited while the other boys held the wire for my brothers so they could carefully return from the forbidden territory.

Losing a frog contest was the last thing on my mind as all six of us ran back home. I had broken a promise to my mother and had been caught in the act. I knew I deserved a spanking and was prepared to receive one.

I was trying to hold back the tears, but the pain of the wound and the broken promise overcame me and I started crying. My brothers and friends seemed concerned as the blood soaked though my white T-shirt and made an ever-widening bright red splotch on my back. As we approached the house I was shocked to see my mother standing in the front yard as though she knew something had happened.

"Mother, I'm sorry I disobeyed you," I said. "I broke my promise. We tried to chase a big frog on the other side of the railroad fence and I cut myself on the wire," I explained.

My mother lifted the back of my shirt and replied, "I think you'll be alright, Timmy. Come on in and we'll clean out your cut." She took my hand in hers and led me into the safety of our home, where she cleaned and bandaged the wound.

When she was finished, I hugged my mother and began to whimper. "I'm sorry," I said. "You were right. We shouldn't have disobeyed you. It won't happen again," I assured.

"I forgive you, Timmy," my mother replied.

Neither my mother nor my father punished me for breaking my promise and disobeying my mother. I guess they thought I had been punished enough. Although the wound did not require stitches, the barbed wire left a small jagged scar on my back that is still visible a half-century later. I occasionally look at it in the mirror to remind myself of the result of a broken promise and the tender love, care and forgiveness my mother showed me that sunny spring day.

The neighbor boys won the frog contest by default. My brothers and I won a far more valuable prize that day. We learned the wisdom of the biblical mandate: "Children, obey your parents in the Lord, for it is right." (Ephesians 6:1)

Entry 8

Polio Pioneers

1953–54—Wichita, Kansas

The summer of 1953 was a fearful time. Tens of thousands of people, mostly children, contracted the dreaded disease polio. The cause of the disease or how it was contracted was a mystery.

Polio often caused weakness and even complete paralysis of arms and legs. If patients survived the poliovirus they often remained confined to wheelchairs or were able to walk only with the aid of braces and/or crutches. In the worst cases polio attacked the diaphragm and patients were placed in large machines called iron lungs that forced air in and out of their weakened or debilitated lungs. Many thousands of children and adults did not survive the disease.

Parents of school-age children were especially frightened by the disease that, for some yet unknown reason, was most prevalent in August. That summer my parents stopped letting us go to the Saturday matinee show at the movie theater for fear we might contract the disease from other kids.

In August of 1953 my oldest brother Steve was nearly 11 years old. I always looked up to my older brother and always wanted to do whatever he was doing. However, because he is three years older than I, he was running while I was still crawling. When I was learning to walk, he was riding a tricycle. When

I was riding a tricycle, he was riding a bicycle. He was always doing things I was too young to do. I idolized Steve and followed him around like a puppy at every opportunity. However, due to our difference in age I spent most of my time playing with Bill, who was only eighteen months younger, and Phil, who was three years younger than me. At the time, my mother was pregnant with my brother Dan.

Steve was happy, outgoing, active and rarely sick. However, that August he came down with a fever accompanied by headaches, upset stomach, sore leg muscles and a stiff neck. These were the classic symptoms of polio. With the onset of these symptoms my mother called Dr. Friesen, who had been our family doctor for many years and had delivered all of my brothers and me.

After hearing the symptoms, Dr. Friesen told my mother Steve needed to go to Wesley Hospital as soon as possible. My father, who at the time worked as a delivery man for Meadow Gold Milk Company, had just finished his early morning milk delivery route and stopped by on his way back to the milk plant to check on Steve.

My mother informed him of the doctor's instructions, and she already had packed a bag for Steve.

My parents awakened my younger brothers and me and informed us that Steve might have polio and that we needed to get up and see him before he left for the hospital.

I could tell my parents were extremely concerned and although my brothers and I were young we knew how serious it could be if Steve had contracted polio.

Tears streamed down my mother's face as we went to the couch by the front door where Steve was lying down. Steve's smile belied his pain and fear. We all hugged Steve and told him we would be praying for him. He was shaking with the chills from his fever, yet his skin felt hot to the touch. I was worried.

My father wrapped a blanket around Steve, took him in his arms and carried him out to the round-nosed Meadow Gold milk truck parked in our driveway with the motor running. My father set Steve on an upside-down metal milk crate he had placed on the floor beside the driver's seat and then slid the right side door shut. Bill, Phil and I stood clustered around my mother on the front porch and waved to Steve and my father. The door on the driver's side of the truck was open, and my father and Steve both waved as they pulled away from our home en route to the hospital. Tears filled my eyes as I stood on the porch and wondered if I would ever see my kind, protective big brother again.

Our worst fears were confirmed when tests showed that Steve in fact had contracted polio. It was especially scary because we did not know how Steve caught the disease or if the rest of us might contract it as well.

I don't remember how long Steve stayed at Wesley Hospital, but it seemed like months. His symptoms grew steadily worse, and he lost strength in both of his legs and couldn't walk. My brothers and I were too young to visit Steve in the hospital and he was isolated from visitors because no one was certain how easily the disease might be communicated to others.

At one point Steve was placed near a boy in an iron lung. A mirror was positioned at an angle above the boy's head so he could see the medical personnel and others who attended to his needs.

"I could see the boy's face in the mirror, and I watched him die," Steve told me later. "I'll never forget the look on his face."

Steve was fortunate, and the disease did not impair his ability to breathe like it did many of the patients. Thousands of young patients did not survive, and many thousands more were left crippled for life.

Each night before bedtime my parents would kneel with us beside our beds and we would all pray that God would spare Steve's life and that he would return home without permanent paralysis.

After a lengthy stay in the hospital, Steve's condition slowly improved. He finally was allowed to come home from the hospital to make room for new polio victims. While he was in the hospital he had been showered with gifts from his brothers, parents and other relatives, but he could only bring home the few items that could be sterilized. All the other gifts, including many comic books, were incinerated by the hospital to prevent the possible spread of the disease to our family and others.

The only present I remember he was allowed to bring home was a Casper the Ghost inflatable and washable vinyl punching bag with sand molded into the bottom for ballast.

During his hospital stay Steve bonded with many of the nurses, doctors and technicians who gave him intensive and loving care. Their interaction and concern profoundly affected his life and helped him determine his lifelong career.

It was a day for celebration when Steve returned from the hospital. He was on crutches and had braces on his legs to help him walk. "Steve, are you glad to be home from the hospital?" I inquired as I placed my arm around him and his wooden crutches. "Was it scary to be there?"

"Timmy, it's great to be home, but the doctors and nurses in the hospital were wonderful to me," he explained. "I was in a lot of pain and sometimes it was scary, but God helped me to get through it. In some ways it was kind of fun getting all of that attention. I know what I'm going to be when I get older," he declared with great certainty. "I'm going to be a doctor and take care of people like the doctors and nurses took care of me!"

For many months Steve went to physical therapy for the famous Kenny treatment named after the nurse who developed the therapy. The treatment called for army blankets or towels that were cut into strips, soaked in hot water and wrapped around the affected limbs. Exercise also was prescribed for the affected limbs. The treatments and exercises—including swimming—eventually increased the flexibility and strength in Steve's legs until he was finally able to shed the leg braces.

Not long after Steve returned from the hospital the radio and newspapers were filled with wonderful news of a new vaccine for polio developed by Dr. Jonas Salk. What caught my family's attention was that Salk needed to have mass testing of the new vaccine before it could be declared effective as a a nationwide preventative for polio.

During 1954, the new experimental vaccine was administered to more than 1.7 million schoolchildren. My school, Levy Elementary, was chosen as one of the test sites for the vaccine. We brought home permission slips for our parents to sign that would allow us to take part in the medical trials. The permission note was specific and warned that although the vaccine was made from a dead poliovirus that was thought to be safe, participants in the vaccine trial risked a possibility of contracting polio. One batch of bad vaccine manufactured by one company infected more than 100 children with polio and resulted in 11 deaths. However, the fear of leaving polio unchecked to kill and maim thousands more was a far more ominous threat.

My parents asked Bill and me if we would like to participate in the trials. They said we would be able to help doctors to help others who might be far less fortunate than our brother Steve.

Bill and I agreed to participate. Our teachers explained how the vaccine worked and told us we were helping to make medical history. After being vaccinated, each child was given a small certificate and a red and white lapel pin imprinted with the words "Polio Pioneer." As I remember, the pin also had small pictures of a hypodermic needle and a microscope.

POLIO PIONEER

My brothers and I and the other children at our school who participated in the trials wore the pins for many months with great pride. The massive medical trials proved the effectiveness of the vaccine against polio. From 1952-54, 100,000 cases of polio were reported in the United States. In 1957 fewer than 6,000 cases of polio were reported nationally. I kept the small "Polio Pioneers" lapel pin for many years. It was lost after my move to Tennessee as an adult.

In 1957 Dr. Albert Sabin developed an oral vaccine that replaced the Salk vaccine. My brothers and I were among the first children in the country to be revaccinated with the colorful sweet liquid dispensed in small paper containers or on sugar cubes. In 1964, the year I graduated from high school, only 121 cases of polio were reported in the United States.

A few months before Steve turned 12, my father became a district circulation manager for a newspaper, *The Wichita Eagle*. Boys normally were not allowed to start throwing papers until they were 12, but Steve was an exception because my father was his supervisor. The walking paper route, which started about two miles from our house, proved to be great physical and mental therapy for Steve. After a year walking his route, his limp completely disappeared.

Steve talked often about his desire to become a doctor, even after we moved to Salina. During his teenage years Steve continued to harbor his dream of a career in medicine, but his courses in auto mechanics and his employment at an auto body shop did little to prepare him for college.

At age 17 Steve's dream of a medical career seemed impossible as continual disagreements with my father came to a breaking point. My father forced Steve to leave our home in Salina and he went to live with our maternal grandparents in Wichita, Kansas.

The Wichita Eagle again played an important role in Steve's life when my grandfather, who had worked as pressman for the *Eagle* for nearly 50 years, got Steve a job as an apprentice pressman.

Steve worked nights at the *Eagle* and attended Wichita State University during the day. He became certified as a medical technologist. His medical certification allowed him to finance his studies in pre-medicine at Oklahoma Baptist University. In 1969 he was admitted to the Kansas City College of Osteopathic Medicine and graduated four years later. He has been a family practice physician in Wichita since 1973, dispensing loving care and healing to his many patients.

Over the years Steve has continually credited his faith in God and his bout with polio for creating in him the desire to emulate the love of God and the love and hands-on care of the physicians, nurses and technicians who rescued him from the grips of polio so many years ago. The investment of love and care in Steve by medical personnel at Wesley hospital in 1954 is a constant reminder to me that our best investments are in the lives of people. Striving for excellence everyday at work has the potential to change the course of people's lives. Loving God and sharing His love with others through consistent acts of care and kindness yield far greater dividends than high-interest savings accounts, blue chip stocks or gold coins locked away in bank deposit boxes.

Entry 9

The Pitchfork

1959—Salina, Kansas

True friendship is a rare and priceless commodity in life. Proverbs 18:24 says "A friend sticks closer than a brother" (NLT). My four brothers and I often have experienced the bond between brothers that the Bible uses to define true friendship.

Whenever I read that verse I think back to an incident that happened when I was 13 and my brother Bill was 12.

When we were growing up, Bill was a daredevil and enjoyed teasing and picking fights. My other brothers and I always accused Bill of getting us in trouble with our father. We knew we should expect to deal with my father and the justice of his wide belt when he caught us fighting or disobeying the rules.

My father operated the *Wichita Eagle* newspaper distributorship for Salina, Kansas, and all my brothers and I had early morning bicycle paper routes beginning in the summer before we entered the fifth grade. We were up at 5 a.m. seven days a week to throw our papers.

We earned about $4 per week throwing papers and received an additional $5 or $6 a month collecting the monthly subscription fee from our 40 to 60 customers. Mailing a payment to the newspaper was unheard of in those days. People preferred to pay their paperboy in person so they could praise or complain about their service. We made additional money by signing up new subscribers.

The money we earned was an important part of my family's income. My parents encouraged us to save for items we needed or wanted. We bought a lot of our own clothes and we all had Schwinn bicycles that we had purchased with our own money. We rode our bicycles to throw papers.

Bill saved his earnings and bought a chestnut brown walking horse named Nancy. She was swaybacked, and we later discovered she was more than 20 years old. Few 12-year-olds could purchase and board even an old swayback horse with money they earned on a paper route.

Bill boarded Nancy at the fairgrounds a few miles from our house. Owning a horse and boarding it in a small 12-foot square stall requires daily cleaning and replenishment of water, hay, grain and bedding straw.

One week our cousin Don from Goddard, Kansas, came to visit us. Don wanted to see Bill's horse, and we were eager to oblige.

My parents rarely took us anywhere by car. We usually rode our bikes or walked. Our garage always contained an extra bicycle or two, so Don, Bill, and my 10-year-old brother Phil and I jumped on our bikes and rode off to the stables.

When we arrived, we tied Nancy outside the stall and began grooming her and cleaning the stable. Phil and I didn't enjoy helping Bill with the cleaning, but we knew that was the price we had to pay to ride Nancy.

Bill, in his usual rambunctious mood, began tossing manure-soiled hay at me as we worked. He and I both were using pitchforks, which were most efficient for loading the old straw into a wheelbarrow and spreading new replacement straw.

"Bill, if you don't stop throwing horse manure on me, I'm going to stab you with this pitchfork," I warned. This only encouraged Bill to continue to see how far he could push me.

"I'm warning you," I said. "I'll stab you if you don't stop right now."

Cousin Don didn't like the pungent odor of the stables, but he was enjoying the show Bill was putting on for him and he egged Bill on.

Finally I'd had enough. I raised my pitchfork in self-defense and lunged at Bill a few times to show him I meant business. He stopped for a while, but as soon as I turned my back I felt a wet plop on the back of my neck.

I turned again in an aggressive offense and backed Bill into a corner with my four-pronged poker. Once cornered, Bill reloaded his pitchfork with new ammo. I responded with a long graceful lunge that speared his pitchfork before glancing off and stabbing Billy solidly in his side. Bill was as shocked as I.

"Oh, Bill, I didn't mean to stab you! I'm sorry!" I yelled. Bill quickly lifted his bloody T-shirt to expose his wounds. When he saw the blood trickling down his side, I thought he was going to faint.

Instantly Don screamed, "I'm going to tell Uncle Alfred and Aunt Lucille what you've done, Tim."

Don shot out of the stall and barely missed being trampled by a startled Nancy, who had been enjoying a meal from her grain bucket. Don grabbed my new bicycle and took off.

"Stop! Don, don't go. Bill's all right." I yelled. Bill, Phil and I looked at each other in sheer panic. We turned and ran as fast as we could after Don. We knew if Don told our dad what had happened we all would be in deep trouble.

The faster we ran and the louder we screamed, the faster Don pedaled. On foot we were no match for my new red and silver Schwinn bicycle with whitewall touring tires.

As Don pedaled out of sight, Bill, Phil and I prepared for my Dad's impending arrival. We quickly removed Bill's bloody shirt and examined his wounds closely. He had suffered two bleeding puncture wounds and one purple puncture. We washed the wounds with a garden hose, and within minutes the bleeding stopped. I was worried about tetanus from the dirty pitchfork until I remembered Bill had received a tetanus shot after a mishap on his bicycle earlier in the year.

Meanwhile Don arrived at our home after nearly being hit by a car. He burst into the house where my parents were preparing a meal. Gasping for air after his emergency ride at breakneck speed, and on the brink of tears, he shouted, "Uncle Alfred, Uncle Alfred, Timmy has stabbed Billy with a pitchfork and there are four holes with blood just a spurtin' out of every hole! Please come quick."

Minutes after Don left we heard a loud crunching sound as the tires of my father's Studebaker station wagon skidded to a stop on the dirt and gravel alleyway outside the stall. The car door slammed shut and we could hear my father's feet pounding the ground as he raced toward the stall. Dad appeared in the doorway, beads of sweat rolling down his forehead.

Inside the stall all was serene. Phil was quietly spreading clean straw on the stall floor while Bill and I were leaning casually against the back wall of the stall, our arms around each other's neck, grinning like Cheshire cats.

"Tim, what in the devil did you do to Bill?" Dad shouted. We could see the concern and anger etched on his face.

"What are you talking about?" Bill and I answered in unison.

"Don said you were both fighting and Timmy stabbed Billy and blood was spurting out of four holes in Billy's side," my Dad replied.

"Well, we tried to stop Don," I said calmly as I pointed to Bill's shirtless torso. "As you can see there are only two holes and no blood is coming from either of them."

"It was just an accident," Bill added. "Tim didn't mean to stab me, we were just jokin' around."

My dad seemed greatly relieved, and his frown relaxed into a slight smile.

"I guess your cousin exaggerated a little," Dad replied. "You boys scared your mother and me half to death. Finish up here and get on home. Lunch is almost ready."

As our dad slid into the station wagon and headed home we congratulated each other with slaps on the back and breathed sighs of relief. We had escaped almost certain punishment and emerged victorious!

When we got home for lunch, Cousin Don, not used to such goings on, had already called his parents. They arrived later that afternoon to take him home—three days early. He never stayed overnight at our home again!

Although my brothers and I had more scraps and scrapes than I can count, we have had a blood bond between us that no one can break.

Our brotherly bond was forged over many years of love—through good times and bad, through sickness and health, through obedience and disobedience, through failures and successes and through laughter and tears.

My four brothers and I can testify that "A friend that sticks closer than a brother," (no pun intended) is a friend indeed!

Entry 10

Thanksgiving Dinner
1958—Salina, Kansas

The October night air was crisp, and the sky was blazing with colors from the setting sun. Leaves that had fallen from the trees crunched and rustled underfoot. The fall weather was invigorating, but the task assigned to my brother, Bill and I was not.

Bill was 11 and I was 12, and it was solicitation night. Each Tuesday my father sent us out with other newspaper carriers to build the family business by selling subscriptions to *The Wichita Eagle*.

My father loaded the station wagon with boys and newspapers. We worked in teams. My father gave each of us a handful of sample copies of the *Eagle* and dropped us off to work the houses in a two- or three-block area.

The other news carriers were there by choice to earn money for selling subscriptions. Sometimes they kept their routes for several years, sometimes for only a few weeks or days as the reality of waking up at 5 a.m. seven days a week to throw newspapers in fair weather or foul took its toll.

We were there because we had no choice. It was part of our required duties as members of the Fields family. When it was time to throw our papers, we couldn't call in sick because it was raining hard or snowing. Even worse, after we threw our own route

51

we had to throw the routes of boys who had called in sick or had quit, not wanting to face snow or subzero temperatures.

As my father let us out of the station wagon on Tuesday evenings, each carrying an armload of papers, we grumbled as we began our task of interrupting the quiet evening of residents of those suburban homes.

We never knew what kind of reception we would receive after we knocked on a door or rang a doorbell.

One thing in our favor was the superior newspaper product tucked under our arms. As the door opened we would greet the resident with a smile and hand him or her a sample copy of the *Eagle*. It always helps to give a free sample of the product before starting a sales pitch.

"Hello Ma'am" or "Hello Sir," we would begin. "I am with the *Wichita Eagle* and I would like to give you a sample copy of the finest newspaper in Kansas.

"*The Eagle* features the latest in state, national and international news provided by reporters and photographers throughout Kansas and, unlike the local paper, the *Eagle* subscribes to the Associated Press and United Press International news services.

"*The Eagle* also features the complete listings of the New York Stock Exchange and is the only newspaper available in Salina that features the 'Peanuts' comic strip."

If the resident was a woman, we would add, "Ma'am, *The Eagle* provides special features for women, including fashions, cooking and family living." If a man came to the door, we would add, "Sir, *The Eagle* has a comprehensive sports section with statewide and national sports scores, and our Sunday paper includes eight pages of full-color comics."

"You can have this newspaper delivered to your front porch each morning before 7 a.m., seven days a week for only $2.80 a month."

If the resident seemed interested but reluctant we would sweeten our sales pitch by concluding, "If you sign up tonight we will give you a one-week free trial subscription beginning in the morning. If you are not completely satisfied you can call and cancel and owe nothing. Would you like to sign up tonight?" we would ask.

In most sales attempts we were turned away with no order or we were interrupted in the middle of our sales pitch with "Sorry, we are not interested," or "We already take *The Salina Journal*. We don't need another newspaper." In about one out of 10 to 15 cases we would make a sale. It was a good feeling, and the $1.40 (half of a monthly subscription price) we received for selling the subscription was excellent pay for a pre-teenager in 1958. I often was designated "high man" for the night and regularly sold three to four subscriptions in a one- to two-hour period.

My father would make his way between the two-boy crews encouraging those who hadn't made a sale, congratulating those who had and restocking us with sample issues of the paper. If we worked quickly we would run out of sample copies of the paper before my father made it back to replenish our supply. When that happened we would sit on the curb and talk. Bill sometimes hastened his rest time by throwing some of his sample copies into a resident's trash can and making his way to the end of the block to wait for my father. Bill rarely received "high man" status when the night's solicitation ended.

As we finished soliciting our last block of houses one evening, Bill and I sat down on the curb of one of the busiest streets in Salina. As we expressed gratitude that our solicitation efforts were finished for the week, a large truck loaded with cages of turkeys roared past us. As it did it bounced over a bump in the street and one of the cages crashed to the ground. The truck didn't stop. Either the driver didn't realize he had lost part of his load or he didn't care. We leapt to our feet as shattered pieces of the cage slid past us. In the darkness a street light illuminated the cloud of dust rising from the place where the cage had fallen. We were shocked to see a large brown turkey staring at us as he stood in the middle of the busy street. Lights from several approaching cars alerted us to the precarious plight of the poor dazed fowl.

Without saying a word we both jumped into action. I had never seen a live turkey up close and the bird was much larger than I had imagined. We grabbed the turkey around his middle, pinning his wings to his body, as we both quickly carried the heavy bird to the curb out of harm's way.

"What are we going to do now?" I asked.

"We can keep him and cook him for Thanksgiving dinner," Bill replied. A few minutes later my father arrived and bounded from the car with a look of astonishment.

We explained what happened, and our dad helped us load the turkey into the back of the station wagon. We held him tightly all the way home.

My mother was a farm girl, and she knew a few things about poultry. She agreed to let us keep our newfound pet, at least for a few weeks.

"He will make a great Thanksgiving dinner," Bill again asserted.

"I don't think so," I replied. "He'll just be our pet."

The first night we secured our new acquisition by tying a piece of twine from one of his legs to a stake in the backyard. We gave him a bowl of water and some bread crumbs to eat. I stretched a piece of old fencing around him to keep our dog and the neighborhood dogs from bothering him.

The next day after school we rode our bicycles downtown to the local feed store where we bought five pounds of chicken feed for 50 cents and returned home to give him a good meal.

We constructed a more permanent cage by stretching wire between our garage and a board fence at the back of our property. For five weeks we fed "Tom" large meals of chicken feed made from cracked wheat, milled oats and crushed kernels of dried yellow corn.

I enjoyed taking care of Tom, who gained several pounds and strutted around his pen, often spreading his tail feathers and expanding his already enormous body, especially when our dog Muggsy would come near the pen.

Two days before Thanksgiving, the dreaded day arrived. My mother came to the pen as I was feeding Tom.

"Tim, it's time," my mother said.

"Time for what?" I hesitantly asked.

"Time to prepare Tom for our Thanksgiving dinner," she replied.

"Mom, please let me keep him. I don't want to eat him," I begged.

"Tim, you know that's not practical. Do you want to help?" my mother asked. "No, you'll have to butcher him yourself," I replied sadly as I walked away.

My mother used her farming skills to prepare Tom for the family table. As we sat down for Thanksgiving Dinner I sadly realized that Tom's fate was the same as all the turkeys he shared a truck ride with only a few weeks earlier.

I have to admit he was the largest, best looking turkey my family ever served for a Thanksgiving meal. Before we began the meal, my father thanked God for providing the food on the table—especially the fine turkey!

The lettuce and tomato salad, mashed potatoes, gravy, dressing, green beans, and cherry pie were delicious. My family said the turkey was the most juicy and tender they had ever eaten. I couldn't say. It was the first and last turkey-free Thanksgiving I ever experienced.

Entry 11

Seventeen Cigars

1958–59—Salina, Kansas

Each summer my father sponsored a contest for his 15 to 20 *Wichita Eagle* newspaper carriers. In return for selling 12 subscriptions to the *Eagle*, each eligible carrier received a trip to Joyland amusement park in Wichita, Kansas, the home of the largest roller coaster in several states.

The one-day trip began after lunch on Friday and included a 90-minute drive to Wichita and a tour of the *Wichita Eagle* newsroom, press room and circulation department.

Then we had supper at a small diner on Pawnee Avenue a short distance from Joyland. I always ordered half of a fried chicken and a large order of french fries.

The contest usually started the first week of July and concluded a week or so before school started. Some carriers took nearly two months to sell 12 subscriptions in door-to-door solicitation.

Those who sold more subscriptions received extra spending money to use during the trip.

If a carrier reported to the weekly solicitation but needed encouragement in selling, my father often went with him until he sold a subscription and then gave the boy credit. This on-the-job training provided both sales instruction and encouragement. Sometimes he sent new carriers with me during solicitation so I could train them. When I sold subscriptions he instructed me to give the sale to the new carriers but secretly gave me credit as well.

The boy with the highest number of sales for the night often received a $1 bonus or some other prize such as a flashlight or pocket knife. My father always concluded the evening of solicitation with cold soft drinks.

Even with sales training, a free subscription or two and weekly prizes, not all of the carriers won the trip to Joyland. If more boys than could fit in our station wagon earned the trip my father took the first load of boys one week and then took a second load when the rest of the crew had sold enough subscriptions to earn the trip.

I always looked forward to the annual Joyland contest because it was the one time each year we boys were allowed to smoke cigars. My father, who never smoked, always told my brothers and me that he didn't want us to smoke, but if we did, he wanted us to do it in front of him and not behind his back.

One summer my brothers and I decided to test my father's challenge to us on smoking and asked him if we could smoke cigars during our trip to Wichita.

"You can smoke as many cigars as you want in the car on the way to Wichita," he replied. "Just don't smoke inside the *Wichita Eagle* building, the restaurant or the amusement park," he warned.

That summer as we left for Joyland with eight boys and my father crammed into our Studebaker Commander wagon, my brothers Phil and Bill, made sure we were in the rear-facing third seat of the wagon with the tailgate window flipped up.

As soon as the wheels began to roll we lit our first cigars. The car was not air conditioned, and the other open windows of the car forced the smoke straight out the back.

We waited for our father's reaction. He was good to his word and took it all in stride. When we began to feel queasy, we stopped smoking. The first year, Bill smoked two cigars and

Phil and I each smoked three. One or two of the other carriers joined us in smoking the smelly stogies but most thought we were crazy and complained about the smell.

The second year my father sponsored the Joyland contest my brothers and I began preparing for the trip well in advance.

Throughout that summer we purchased packages of inexpensive cigars at the local drugstore. Then we sneaked off to the river or the horse stables where Bill kept his horse, and smoked one or two cigars a week.

We never seemed to have trouble buying the cigars. If the store clerks asked, we told them we were buying them for our father. At the beginning of the summer Phil and I challenged each other to a cigar-smoking contest to see who could smoke the most cigars during our upcoming trip to Joyland.

Several times as we returned from our secret cigar-smoking sessions our mother asked us why we smelled like smoke. "Have you boys been smoking?" she asked.

"They were smoking at the barber shop," we replied, or "Some men at the fairgrounds were smoking when we went to feed Bill's horse."

"I hope you boys aren't smoking those nasty cigars," my mother said. "They make you smell like an outhouse and they are bad for you." In subsequent smoking outings we wore jackets to protect our clothes from the smell and removed the coats before coming home. On the way home, we would also wash our hands and face and chew gum to hide the smell of smoke.

That summer my brothers and I crossed a line. Instead of a one-time challenge or a yearly ritual we enjoyed smoking the cigars on a regular basis. We liked their sweet smell and taste before they were lit. If we went too long between smokes we could feel the nicotine beckoning to us. Although we didn't intentionally inhale the cigars, we inhaled the secondary smoke and ingested traces of nicotine directly into our mouths.

As the day approached for our second annual Joyland trip, my bothers and I were ready for the cigar smoking-contest. We had stocked up on cigars and began puffing on our first ones as we pulled out of our driveway on the way to Wichita.

We puffed hard on the cigars, racing to finish one and start the next. During the 90-mile ride to Wichita, Bill, Phil and I each smoked four cigars. We were in a dead heat. Our mouths were numb and we were feeling lightheaded. Before our tour of the *Eagle* we washed our hands and faces and chewed gum to try to hide the smell from the cigars. Since we had toured the *Eagle* plant the year before, Bill, Phil and I left the tour after our visit to the pressroom and went outside to each smoke a fifth cigar. Bill started looking green and decided to quit the competition. As the other carriers loaded into the car, Phil and I each smoked our sixth cigar. I was woozy, but Phil seemed fine. By the time we finished our cigars we were at the restaurant. We all piled out of the car. It felt good to walk around and get a breath of fresh air. "How are you doing, Phil?" I asked.

"I'm a little lightheaded," he replied. "Maybe I'll feel better after I eat."

As we sat down to order I felt nauseated and I was dizzy. I quickly ordered my chicken dinner and took a few drinks of a cold soft drink.

"I think I'm going to be sick," I told Phil, "I'm going outside."

I struggled to make it out the door. I walked to the car and lay down in the back seat. I had never felt so sick in my life.

All I could think was how stupid I had been to work all summer for this trip and then make myself too sick to eat that delicious fried chicken dinner and ruin my visit to Joyland.

As I lay there in agony I promised God if he would help me feel well enough to eat the meal and make it to Joyland I would never smoke another cigar again. I knew I probably shouldn't be praying such a selfish prayer, but I did it anyway.

My insides felt like they were going to explode, and as I got out of the car, I threw up. I breathed large gulps of the fresh night air, and my head began to clear. I was still wobbly, but I made it back inside. Most of the carriers were eating fried chicken and french fries with fresh rolls and honey or double decker hamburgers. One boy was enjoying a grilled cheese sandwich and a large chocolate malt. The food didn't look appealing, but

I was determined not to let my chicken go to waste. I asked the waitress if she would put it in a sack to go.

I sat still through the rest of the meal and drank long sips of a cold Coke. My father came over to inquire if I was alright and then asked me what was wrong.

"I smoked too many cigars," I admitted. "I think I've ruined my trip."

He smiled and said, "Well, maybe you'll feel better later."

Bill and Phil seemed to feel much better than I did, but they were eating a little slower than usual. As we loaded back into the car for our trip to Joyland I felt much better. My empty stomach was calling for something to eat, and a few minutes after I arrived at Joyland I sat on a bench and slowly relished the dinner I couldn't eat at the diner. I felt even better after finishing the meal but decided I would stay off the roller coaster and most of the other rides.

Phil decided he'd had enough cigars for the night, too. He and I were even at six cigars each and agreed to end the contest in a tie.

Phil, Bill and I spent most of our time playing skeetball and other games of skill that night and avoided the motion rides. I thanked God for redeeming the evening for me and remembered my promise to Him. I never smoked another cigar as a child.

I eventually broke my promise nearly 20 years later. Once every year or so my four brothers and I try to get together for a reunion. Bill, Phil and I sometimes enjoy a good quality cigar at these reunions. My oldest brother Steve and my youngest brother Dan don't share in this ritual.

"It's all right Tim," Phil assures. "This cigar won't make you sick. It's a mild one. I picked it out just for you."

We mingle our cigar smoking with cups of strong gourmet coffee. As the thick smoke curls above us we reminisce about the good old days when life was simpler and when, in one afternoon, the three of us together smoked 17 cigars in five hours and lived to tell about it.

Entry 12

Strap City

1953–1960—Salina, Kansas

In a household of five boys with only an 11-year range in age, discipline was not only desired but required. My four brothers and I were neither ill-mannered nor unusually disobedient but we were full of energy, curiosity and sometimes bad judgment.

Our playing and teasing sometimes ended in roughhousing, wrestling and even fights. Our mother usually meted out the punishment for less serious offenses. A disappointed look or verbal reprimand for wrestling or fighting, a taste of Ivory soap on tongue and teeth for a dirty word, or an occasional whack on the backside or even simply a threat of one for more serious disobedience such as sassing our mother was usually all it took for our mother to keep us in line.

Our mother was our friend and confidant, and she knew and we knew that my father's form of punishment was always more harsh and often crossed the line between punishment and abuse.

On rare occasions when we boys had an unusually serious fight or when someone broke something and wouldn't confess to the misdeed my mother would say, "When your father gets home he will have to deal with this." On other occasions my father would catch us in the act of disobedience, and he would immediately punish us.

We boys called this type of punishment by my father "going to strap city." The punishment was aptly named because our dad used a two-inch-wide leather belt to deliver the punishment.

If we had ample warning we would run upstairs and put on several pairs of underwear or two pairs of jeans. If the offense was particularly grave, we would stuff comic books in the seat of our pants.

Whichever son was receiving punishment would be sent or escorted to one of the upstairs bedrooms. The drill was the same for all my brothers and me. For example, when I was on the punishment line I would bend over and grab my ankles and clench my teeth as the strap whizzed through the air and cracked sharply against my backside. If more than one of us were the culprits, we would have some company in the punishment line. Along with the sting of the strap, the force of the blow seemed to lift us off our feet as we quickly braced for a second, third or fourth blow. A one-lash punishment was never an option. Lingering red welts on legs and behind were a reminder to stay within the boundaries next time we were tempted to stray or disobey.

As my brothers and I wrestled, argued and fought we would yell out to the offending brother, "If you don't stop it, you are going to strap city!" The threat of such a visit often would bring a wayward brother back to his senses.

On several occasions one of my brothers or I broke something and then would not admit who had broken it. In such cases my father would sentence all of us to strap city. We often knew or suspected who the offender was but our loyalty as brothers usually prevented us from telling on each other.

My dad would line us up from the oldest to the youngest. My youngest brother Dan was excused from the line-up because of his age. Then we would all simultaneously bend over and grab our ankles.

"I'm going to go down the line and give each one of you a lash with my belt until the guilty party confesses," my Dad would announce in his gruffest voice. "If whoever did this will confess, you will spare your brothers from punishment, and I'll give you only four more lashes of the belt," he would explain. "Otherwise you'll be here the rest of the night."

My father would then proceed to go down the line doling out one lash after another. We could hear the strap whiz through the air and stop with a sharp crack each time it made contact with the backside of a brother in crime. As each brother received his punishment, the rest of us would cringe as if we were being hit simultaneously. It was a point of honor not to yell out as our bodies absorbed the sting of the strap. Sometimes on the second or third round as our will wore down, we couldn't help but let out a yelp. If I or any brother but Bill was the offending party, the confession usually came early, sometimes even before the first round of blows.

However when Bill had committed the offense we knew we were all in trouble. My dad could have cut off Bill's right hand or tortured him with fire, and he wouldn't confess.

I remember well the time Bill broke a window by throwing a shoe in anger. Neither he nor we would tell who had committed the offense.

Subsequently, my brothers and I found ourselves at the familiar doorstep to "strap city," and we lined up for our corporate punishment ritual. When I saw the smile on Billy's face, I surmised, *Billy will never admit to this crime, and we could be here for an eternity, or maybe until my father stops from exhaustion.* A plan began to hatch in my mind. *Whiz, Kerwhap!* The belt struck its first blow on my brother Steve. I braced for the next whizzing sound and the sting of the strap on my behind. As I was lifted into the air from the impact, I yelled out, "Yeoow, I broke the window! I'm the guilty one, Dad."

Billy was shocked at my confession but never let out a peep. My other brothers were shocked as well, but they also were relieved. They remained silent, too.

My father then proceeded to give me four more stinging lashes with his belt.

On several other occasions when we all went to strap city because of Bill, I took the blame. However, I waited until one round of the strap was completed. I wanted Bill to get at least one lash of the strap. The five lashes I received were far better than an unknown number.

My father later told me that several times he knew Billy was the guilty party. "Why didn't you spank him instead of me?" I asked.

"Well, knowing you didn't do it, I didn't spank you that hard," he said.

I thought my father's reasoning was illogical and unjust. His practice of punishing all of his sons for the misbehavior of one has made me intolerant of people who punish groups of people for the wrongs of a few, especially when they know who committed the offense.

Many years later when I was working for a national religious ethics agency, our boss reprimanded the staff for making too many personal calls and tying up the business lines. "Some of you are guilty of this, and you need to limit your calls," he said. Our boss and all of the staff members knew the identity of the guilty party.

This pushed an emotional button from my past, and I blurted out, "If I am the guilty party, I wish you'd come to me in private and tell me."

My boss and the other staff members seemed surprised at my response. As we returned to our offices, my fellow employees warned me I would be in trouble for making the statement. A few minutes after the staff meeting my boss sauntered slowly into my office and sat down. "Now Tim, you know I wasn't talking about you," he said. I proceeded to tell him about my visits to strap city as a kid and told him I was sensitive to group reprimands for the offenses of a few. He seemed to understand.

Not until I began teaching a Sunday School class of senior men, many of whom are 80 or older, did I gain new insight into my father's method of punishment.

One Sunday, I used the example of my brothers' and my wrongdoing and my father's method of punishment to make the point that one person's sin or wrongful actions impacts others, sometimes families, or even nations or the world.

The following week, a medical doctor in my class told me that he had discussed my father's form of punishment with fellow physicians.

"Well, what did they think?" I asked.

"What else could your father have done?" the doctor asked in reply. "One of you was guilty of breaking the rules, and the other four were guilty of knowing who committed the offense and covering for your brother," he said. "Your group punishment was the result of not calling your guilty brother to face his judgment," the doctors had concluded.

I had never thought of it that way. Looking at it from the doctors' perspective, my father was illustrating an important life concept. One's actions, both positive and negative, can affect others—sometimes many others. The illegal or unethical practices of a few corporate executives can destroy a multinational company. The illegal or immoral actions of a president of a country can have devastating effects on the economic, social and emotional well-being of a nation.

Our visits to strap city, though feared by my brothers and me, were later modified as a disciplinary tactic by at least one of my brothers. My oldest daughter Tammy, who was 7 years old at the time, told me that while traveling from Wichita, Kansas, to Garfield, Arkansas, with my brother Steve and his family, her three cousins were fighting in the car. Her uncle Steve repeatedly threatened to stop the car and take the boys to "strap city." After many warnings Steve finally pulled the car to the side of the road, lined the three boys across the back bumper of the car and used his belt to bring them to their senses. They too, some 25 years later, still talk about their visits to "strap city."

As a father of three daughters, I'll admit I've sentenced them to strap city but more often with my hand than with my belt. They didn't like corporal punishment any more than I did. However, I never spanked all three girls for the misbehavior of one.

As an adult Tammy is adamant against spanking her two daughters (my granddaughters) and uses "time out" to keep them in line.

Spanking, especially with a belt or green switch, can leave mental images and sometimes scars that last a lifetime, especially if the punishment is excessive or unjust.

Even though my father's method of punishment with the strap and at times with his open hand or fist was usually inappropriate, we knew he loved us and was attempting to teach his sons that we are accountable for our actions and are sometimes adversely affected by the actions even of those we love.

In spite of his often negative examples, my father made his point about the importance of obedience and taking responsibility for one's actions. Both of my parents believed and attempted to practice the biblical admonition of Proverbs 22:6, which states "Train up a child in the way he should go, and when he is old he will not depart from it."

Entry 13

First Kiss

1963–64—Salina, Kansas

The first time a boy kisses a girl in a romantic way is an experience he probably will remember for the rest of his life. My first kiss was no exception. I was a sophomore at Salina High School in Salina, Kansas. It happened on my first bona fide date.

One of my high school classmates introduced me to Cheryl (I have changed her name to protect her from any embarrassment). Our first date was with another couple. We went to the drive-in theatre in my 1960 Ford station wagon. Prior to our first date, Cheryl and I had talked on the phone, and I had taken her home from school several times. I was attracted to Cheryl, and my goal was to kiss her before our first date was over. I escorted Cheryl to my car, and as I walked around the car to enter the driver's side, she slid across the wide front seat to sit close to me. I was encouraged! We picked up the other couple and headed for the drive-in. As the movie started our friends in the back seat were already practicing their obviously well-honed kissing skills.

I placed my arm around Cheryl's shoulder, and she snuggled even closer. The stage was set for success. I waited for the first opportunity to kiss Cheryl. My heart was racing but I was determined. I started to make my move several times but I couldn't get up the nerve. Finally I said to myself, "It's now or never!" I pulled Cheryl closer, and as she turned her face towards mine I kissed her—right on the nose!

I was horrified and embarrassed. I had blown my first kiss! We both laughed—I nervously! Cheryl immediately put her warm hand on my cheek to steady my aim. There were no more misalignments that night or any other time during our courtship. I suspect it was not Cheryl's first kiss. She was a good teacher. Needless to say we spent more time kissing that night than watching the movie. I have no recollection of the movie that was showing.

In spite of my initial missed target, Cheryl was my steady and only girlfriend for the next 18 months. We grew close, and we were a good match. Cheryl was skilled in all the homemaking amenities. She was a good cook and made many of her own clothes. She was smart, witty and, most importantly, we could talk about anything. Cheryl and I discussed family, friends and the future.

As we grew closer, we spent hours talking on the phone or in person at her home or at mine. She lived on South Eighth Street and I lived on South Fifth, so when we wanted to spend time together we could do so on instant notice. On my front porch or hers or in the front seat of the Ford we shared our dreams for vocation, bemoaned problems with parents and siblings and even discussed the possibility of marriage and children. I had no sisters, and Cheryl always skillfully answered my questions about women's mental, physical and psychological qualities.

Although Cheryl was an active member of a United Brethren church and I was a member of a small Southern Baptist church, our theology was basically the same. We both shared a deep and abiding faith in God and had accepted His gift of salvation made possible through His Son Jesus. Cheryl's faith in Christ met the first and foremost qualification I had set for my future wife. We occasionally attended services at each other's church but we each remained active in our own church throughout our courtship.

In my opinion Cheryl and I had a near-perfect relationship. My parents and brothers liked Cheryl, and I sensed that her family liked me.

Toward the end of our 18 months of steady dating, our lives came to a crossroads. Cheryl, although much more intellectual than I and a much better student, wanted to marry and settle into family life. I think she yearned to be a wife, a homemaker and a mother. She was well suited for all three roles.

I planned to enter the printing trade, and as a junior I was in trade printing classes the first three hours of every school day. Our classes printed all of the forms and other printed materials for the Salina Board of Education. The students and the taxpayers alike benefited from the arrangement. Toward the end of our junior year, more than a year after we first started dating, I decided I wanted to go to college.

During our long talks together Cheryl and I not only discussed my affinity for the printing trade but I shared with her my dream of living in the mountains of Colorado and writing children's stories. I had dabbled with penning poetry and read some of my poems to Cheryl.

The change in the course of our relationship began in my trade printing class. Each week the journalism students came to read press proofs of the *Salina High News*, our student newspaper.

It was the highlight of the week for our all-male printing class when the members of the journalism class arrived, because many of the female journalists were some of the best looking coeds in school. Whenever an especially curvaceous female journalist brightened the print shop with her presence, we printers motioned with our eyes or hands to alert our fellow tradesmen. It was a vivid social contrast—the white collar journalists in their preppy clothes and the blue collar boys with ink-blackened hands and denim aprons.

One day after the journalism students had completed their proofing and gone back to class, Mr. Robert Caldwell, our printing teacher, made a statement that ultimately changed the course of my life and probably doomed my relationship with Cheryl.

"Those journalism students are all white-collar types," Mr. Caldwell said as I was helping him get the newspaper ready for press. "They don't know what it's like to get their hands dirty."

What a profound statement from a high school teacher who wore brightly colored expensive neck ties, starched dress shirts and cufflinks and in later years was elected the first and only black mayor of Salina, Kansas, for three terms.

I looked down at my ink-soiled hands and thought, *Yes, my hands have been dirty from press ink since I was in the fourth grade.*

My father had been a newspaper distributor for the *Daily Oklahoman* in Lawton, Oklahoma, before my family moved to Salina, where my father built a distribution agency for the *Wichita Eagle* newspaper.

In Lawton I sold Sunday newspapers on the street on Saturday nights when I was in the fourth grade and came home with ink-blackened hands. I was in the fifth grade when we moved to Salina and immediately was assigned a paper route. I came home each morning seven days a week for the next seven years with ink-blackened hands from folding and throwing newspapers.

Mr. Caldwell had no idea of the blowtorch he had lit in my life with his offhand comment. I had to restrain myself from shouting back "I don't want to spend the rest of my life with ink-blackened hands, and I'm not going to!" From that moment my dream to be a writer took center stage in my life. Within a matter of weeks I started planning how I could go to college and become a journalist!

My mom and Cheryl were the first to know about my desire to change my chosen profession from printer to journalist. Both were supportive of my newfound purpose.

I had never before considered attending college, but now I was obsessed with the idea. I had taken no college prep courses, and I would soon be a senior.

After lengthy sessions with the guidance counselor, I mapped

First Kiss   71

out a totally new course for my senior year. I enrolled in courses that soon-to-be seniors had taken while I was in industrial arts learning how to rebuild carburetors and during those three hours each day I spent in printing classes as a junior.

Classes in biology, college preparatory English, German, sociology, American history and journalism necessitated a complete turnabout in my high school career.

Mr. Caldwell seemed devastated when I told him. He had hand-picked me and a few others in the trade printing class and had taught us how to run every piece of equipment in the shop. Only two other printing students had been given the privilege of learning how to run the enormous clanking Linotype machine and the "cutting edge" offset printing presses. My teacher's partial payback for this extra training was to have skilled printers three hours a day during our senior year. In addition to teaching students, Mr. Caldwell was held accountable for all the printed materials requested by the Board of Education!

In spite of my change in career, the printing skills Mr. Caldwell taught me have paid dividends throughout my career in communications and publishing. I am thankful to Mr. Caldwell, who later admitted to my father that he was proud of the decision I had made. I was not surprised to learn years later that Mr. Caldwell went on to serve as a state representative in the Kansas Legislature and was named Kansas Teacher of the Year in 1976.

I didn't know it at the time, but due in part to my new career path, my dating relationship with Cheryl would end in four months. Now, nearly 38 years later, I honestly don't remember all of the details of our dating demise.

A recent rereading of Cheryl's full-page notes in both the 1963 and 1964 *The Trail* yearbooks provided hints. At the close of our junior year Cheryl wrote: *I don't know what I am going to say that I haven't said a million times before. I can't wait until next year when we graduate, and I think you know why. Next year will be rough for both of us but I am pretty sure we will make it together some way.*

Her 1964 full-page entry gave clues to the changes a year can bring: *I have been waiting for this day as I know you have also.*

*I know this day isn't what we once thought it would be and I'm
sorry for that. I hope you have decided it was for the best. I keep
telling myself it was....I hope you know how I feel even if I am a
little confused...Your friend forever, Cheryl.*

In the remaining month of our junior year and the summer
that followed I think Cheryl began to realize my plans for college
were not compatible with marriage soon after graduation. I knew
that I would be lucky to work my way through college even as an
unmarried student. My dreams for the future put any thoughts of
matrimony on the back burner.

This all seemed so logical at the time. I wanted my relationship
with Cheryl to continue, but I was in for a surprise that taught
me how love can quickly turn from bliss to pain.

I felt that Cheryl cared for me deeply, but her dreams and mine
seemed to be at cross purposes. That summer I worked for my father and relieved him from his daily grind of getting up at 3 a.m.
to deliver newspapers to his carriers and to restock the newspaper racks throughout town and at Schilling Air Force Base. My
dates with Cheryl that summer were wonderful respites from the
early morning work.

Sometime during the summer Cheryl was introduced to a
young air traffic controller stationed at the air base who, I think,
was attending her church. I'm sure he saw in Cheryl all of the
wonderful qualities that I enjoyed. Our relationship had already
begun to cool, and we agreed we could date other people.

I didn't expect that decision to drastically affect our relationship,
but I was shocked when I called Cheryl's home one evening and her
mother told me that Cheryl couldn't come to the phone. Cheryl had
never refused to take my calls before and was always at home when
I called. A mutual friend broke the news to me. She told me that
Cheryl was dating the airman and liked him.

With increasing frequency Cheryl declined dates with me, and
her mother made excuses for why Cheryl couldn't come to the
phone. Several times I got in my car and slowly drove past her
Eighth Avenue home. The strange car parked in front of her
house confirmed my fears and tied my stomach in knots.

Some of the most painful hours of my life were spent that

summer lying on the front porch of my home after dark. After talking with Cheryl's mother, who became increasingly terse in informing me that Cheryl wasn't available to talk with me, I would sprawl out on the hard cool concrete of our spacious front porch, sometimes face down and sometimes flat on my back. I still remember the terrible cramping in my stomach, the sense of total rejection and the tears that streamed down my face as I thought of Cheryl in someone else's arms. Sometimes I felt as though I would rather be dead!

My sweet mother helped me through that painful summer. She comforted me and told me not to worry. "God has someone special in mind for you, Tim, and if Cheryl isn't the one, God will help you find that girl when the time is right."

Sometimes when I thought I couldn't stand the pain any longer, my mother would quietly make her way to the front porch, sit down beside me and rub her loving hands across my back or shoulders and wisely say, "Tim, you're in God's hands. Everything will work out. You'll see."

By the first month of our senior year Cheryl and I were no longer dating. We still had a cordial relationship, and my feelings for her were still strong, but I began the healing process by dating other girls. My senior year turned out to be a wonderful turning point in my life. The pain of losing Cheryl soon abated, and my preparation for college was at full tilt. Two months before the close of my senior year, I started dating another wonderful girl who affected my life in far different ways.

At numerous times over the years I have thought about Cheryl. I knew that about a year after we graduated from high school she married the air traffic controller. In fact, several months after our high school graduation, she stopped by my house, bounded out of that beautiful copper-colored 62 Belle Air Chevrolet two-door hardtop to personally announce her engagement. Standing next to that large concrete front porch, she proudly showed me her diamond engagement ring. Cheryl and I were still friends. We had a special bond between us. By then I was totally enamored with my new girlfriend and thanked Cheryl for our time together and wished her the best in her upcoming marriage.

I had no contact with Cheryl for nearly 38 years but often thought of her and thanked God for Cheryl and the wonderful months we spent together planning and dreaming for the future.

In 1969 I found and married the special girl my mother told me God had in mind for me. Although my theology holds that God allows us a free choice in the matter and that any given person has many potential compatible mates, I believe God did lead me to my wife Linda.

I have a wonderful marriage that has yielded three beautiful daughters, two beautiful granddaughters and absolutely no regrets!

In mid-2001 my youngest daughter Becky told me about a website where people could sign up and make contact with other high school classmates who had registered with the service. Neither Cheryl nor my second high school girlfriend were listed with the service. I added my name to the Salina High School class of 1964.

A month later I received an e-mail informing me that a new classmate from 1964 had registered on the site. There I found Cheryl's name. I debated whether or not to send Cheryl an e-mail. *Maybe she wouldn't remember me*, I thought. I decided to take the chance and e-mail her. A few days later Cheryl e-mailed me back. I was delighted but not surprised to learn that after 36 years Cheryl is still married to the former air traffic controller who is now an executive in an international energy company. They have children and grandchildren.

In our exchange of e-mails, we brought each other up to date on nearly four decades of our lives since we parted company. God has wonderfully blessed Cheryl's family and mine as we traveled different roads in life.

This chance contact after many years is meaningful to me, and I consider it a gift from God. In Cheryl's first e-mail she wrote: *Before I update you on my life I need to tell you what a great influence you were to my life. You were a very important part of my spiritual life. You taught me to have faith in God, and that has been so important through the years. I just feel that too often people who make a difference in someone's life never realize it. Thank you!*

Those words brought me to tears. I could have said the exact same thing about Cheryl.

In my e-mail reply I told her that I'd often wondered if people changed from who they were in high school. I told Cheryl it was obvious. She was the same wholesome, God-fearing person at 55 that she had been at 16 and 17.

This update of Cheryl's life was a reaffirmation of my faith in Christ. Cheryl at 17 became the standard by which I measured every girl I dated. Not until I met my wife Linda six years later did I find another woman who could talk with me about anything and who loved God with all her heart, mind, soul and strength.

This entry in the book is due in part to Cheryl's e-mail. Her choice of a lifelong mate was obviously a wise one. Like me, Cheryl found the special person God had in mind for her. I thank God for the wisdom of Cheryl's mother and mine. They both exhibited God's love and care as they encouraged us to seek His will at a crucial crossroads in our young and impressionable lives.

Love at First Sight

1964—Salina, Kansas/Manhattan, Kansas

My work and studies consumed me as I began my senior year of high school. My decision to pursue a career as a journalist and attend college totally changed my high school life. Instead of rifle club and wrestling I became president of the Quill and Scroll Society, sports writer and then news editor of the *Salina High News* and co-anchor of a weekly Salina High news program on KSAL radio. Instead of throwing newspapers for my father I was hired by KSAL radio to edit a newsgram that recapped the morning news in short, concise phrases.

I wrote the newsgram beginning at 6:00 each morning and then delivered copies to area restaurants in a little bright red Plymouth Valiant station wagon emblazoned with large letters that read *KSAL Big Red Mobile News*. I felt like Walter Cronkite, Jr. as I drove the car each morning around Salina. The little red wagon was festooned with police radio antennas and mobile antennas for communication with the station. The police radio constantly crackled inside the car as the police dispatcher communicated with the patrol officers in ten-code language. Occasionally the station's two-way radio crackled out my name as I was summoned from newsgram rounds to return the KSAL Big Red Mobile unit to the station so the news crew could rush to some breaking news event such as a fire or major auto accident.

My editing of the newsgram only lasted a few months, because my poor typing produced a stencil covered with correction fluid that often resulted in a printed newsgram with little black blotches where some of the corrections had been made. Several times the news anchor rescued me by retyping the stencil during commercial breaks or during songs. Although I was praised for the journalistic aspects of my work, I was soon relieved of my newsgram editing and typing duties and replaced by a female college journalism student who could type with great speed and accuracy. The station management asked me to continue to deliver the newsgrams in "Big Red" but I soon quit to return to work throwing newspapers for my father.

My heavy academic load and thrill of working in journalism gave me little time to bemoan my loss of Cheryl as my steady girlfriend. In journalism class I was surrounded by witty, attractive coeds. One especially beautiful and curvaceous journalism coed caught my eye, but she practically had boys lined up around the school waiting to date her. She was a brunette with sultry eyes and a knockout figure. Diane had a younger sister Karen (not their real names) who was a cheerleader and was in pre-publications class—the pre-requisite for the senior journalism course.

The pre-publication students often assisted the senior journalism students much like interns would assist reporters and editors on a commercial newspaper. The first time Diane's little sister Karen entered our journalism classroom I turned to a fellow journalist and asked, "Who is that?"

"It's Diane's little sister," I was informed.

"Beauty certainly runs in that family," I said. "It doesn't seem possible but she's even more beautiful than her sister. I think I'm in love!"

Two months prior to graduation I had the privilege of working with Diane on several special writing projects. One evening after school I called her at home to discuss a project. Her sister Karen answered the phone and summoned Diane. After I had talked several minutes on the phone with her, Diane let out out a loud squeal.

"What's going on?" I asked.

"My sister Karen is throwing shoes at me," Diane replied haltingly.

"Why is she doing that?" I queried.

"She's jealous because I'm talking to you," she replied as the background noise grew louder.

"Now she's throwing pillows at me!" Diane yelled.

I was dumbstruck for a moment. I couldn't believe my ears!

"I didn't know Karen even knew who I was," I replied.

"We'll she does and she wants to go out with you," Diane answered loudly so her sister would be certain to hear.

"You've got to be kidding," I said. "She wants to go out with me?" After I finished the conversation and hung up the phone my head was filled with visions of going out on a date with this beautiful girl. Unlike her sister, Karen had a more petite figure and was quieter and more reserved. She had a wonderful timid smile.

The next day in journalism class I reconfirmed with Diane that her sister Karen was serious about going out on a date with me. That evening, I gathered the courage to call Karen. She answered the phone and recognized my voice. "Oh, just a minute," she replied, "I'll get Diane."

"No, wait, Karen. I didn't call to talk with Diane. I want to talk with you," I said. After a few moments of small talk I asked Karen for a date and she immediately agreed to go out with me.

I drove up to Karen's home "on the hill"—as we referred to the area of upscale homes in Salina where she lived—and she introduced me to her mother, father and little brother. I could tell immediately that Karen and Diane had inherited their mother's beauty.

Karen and I hit it off immediately, and we dated steadily for the remainder of my senior year, throughout the summer and for a short time after I went to college at Kansas State University. From our first date, I felt like one of the luckiest guys in the world. Karen's good looks were only the beginning of her endearing qualities. This cute girl who was smart, kind, loving and gentle was my girlfriend. For me it *was* love at first sight!

Although she was a cheerleader and popular in school, Karen had a shyness that appealed to me. She was down to earth, and our personalities simply clicked in spite of the fact we were from two different social cultures. She had always run with the white-collar kids and I had always identified with blue-collar kids. Most of her friends were rich kids whose parents worked in white-collar professions. Although it didn't seem to phase Karen, it bothered me. If I hadn't been on a path for college and enrolled in journalism, Karen and I never would have met.

My older brother Steve was also dating a girl "on the hill" who ironically lived only a few doors down from Karen. Steve and I both carried the self-imposed stigma of working-class boys dating rich girls. We felt as though our girlfriends' families thought less of us because we were "paperboys" who had a paperboy father! How could my doctor-to-be brother have known he would someday live in houses equal to or better than any house "on the hill" in Salina.

My mother and father readily accepted Karen. My brothers seemed equally impressed with my choice. A little more than a month after our first date Karen experienced a big disappointment in her life that would affect both of us in unexpected and profound ways.

Each year, the cheerleaders were required to try out and compete to remain on the squad. It was almost a formality, and failing to make the squad in succeeding years was a rarity. Karen became the rarity. For reasons many suspected to be political on the part of the teachers who judged the cheerleading tryouts, Karen was not selected to be cheerleader for her junior year. She was devastated. Later that day we made the rounds in her little white Ford Fairmont sport coupe so Karen could be consoled by all of her girlfriends around Salina. Since I had only been dating Karen a short while and most of her friends were sophomores, I didn't know these girls and I felt out of place. I stayed in the car and comforted and encouraged Karen after each tearful encounter with her friends. After a few weeks Karen seemingly put the experience behind her and went on with life.

As the annual junior-senior prom approached, several of my friends asked me to invite a foreign exchange coed to attend the prom with me. No one had asked the exchange student to the prom, and my friends knew Karen was a sophomore and couldn't attend. Karen's sister thought it was a great idea and told Karen to talk me into the date.

When Karen asked me, I told her I couldn't do it and used the convenient excuse that I didn't know how to dance. "I'll teach you," Karen replied. I was both excited and disappointed. I wanted Karen to teach me how to dance, but not so I could date another girl I didn't even know. *How could Karen ask me to do such a thing?* I asked myself. It felt awkward to me. *Doesn't she love me?* I wondered. However, after a few persuasive hugs I reluctantly agreed.

Karen was a wonderful and patient dance teacher. I was a pathetic student. Nevertheless, I took the foreign exchange student to the prom, and she and I endured the night. I tried my best to be gracious and kind but I thought about Karen the entire night and wished I was dancing with her. The exchange student deserved a much better date for the evening.

Even greater than the social differences between Karen and me were our religious backgrounds. Karen's aunt was a devout Catholic nun, but Karen and her family rarely attended church. Unlike the ease and frequency with which Cheryl and I had discussed our faith, I could not bring myself to share my deepest religious feelings with Karen. We talked about church because I attended regularly and Karen knew my faith was extremely important to me. However, unlike Cheryl, I was sure Karen had not made a personal commitment to Christ. I continually thanked God for this girl with whom I was so enthralled, and I prayed that I would have the courage to share my faith with her.

Karen and I spent hours on the phone and dated nearly every weekend. We loved going to the drive-in theatre where Cheryl, my first girlfriend had taught me the fine art of kissing. I loved being with Karen even though our conversations were not as profound and down to earth as those Cheryl and I had shared.

A few weeks after Karen's disappointing failure to make the cheerleading squad I invited her to attend revival services at my small Baptist church. Karen and I attended all four nights of the revival service during the week and she even attended church with me the following Sunday morning. Although I liked our pastor, I felt the revival messages were not up to his usual standards. I was surprised that Karen kept accepting my invitations to attend with me.

In spite of what I considered less-than-brilliant preaching, my pastor did present the simple message found in John 3:16: "For God so loved the world that he gave his only begotten son that whosoever believeth in him shall not perish but shall have everlasting life."

Maybe Karen was faithful in attendance because she was being convicted by the simple truth of that message or maybe it was simply because her parents were out of town part of that week.

Her parents and little brother were still out of town Sunday afternoon, and we found ourselves alone in her home studying for finals on the comfortable couch in Karen's living room. The physical attraction between us was extremely strong, and every time I was alone with Karen it was a constant battle on my part to keep my hormones in check. Karen never refused my advances, and I was the one who would reluctantly put on the brakes. That afternoon we enjoyed long kisses interspersed with English, algebra and world history. In a weak moment my hands wandered and Karen quickly but gently took my hand and said "Tim, this is wrong. I know this isn't what God wants us to do."

That moment is seared into my memory like the mark of a hot branding iron. Karen had suddenly become God's servant, gently but firmly keeping our relationship within His will. At that moment I realized that in spite of my frailties God had given me the opportunity for which I had prayed.

I was nearly euphoric. In the moments that followed I shared with Karen about my faith in Christ and how she too could ask Christ to come into her life and how she could have a personal relationship with God through Christ. Karen was crying, and so was I. Karen prayed, asking God to forgive her of her sins, and asked Christ to come into her life. She claimed the promises shared in those five revival services by a simple Baptist preacher.

I told Karen that although it wasn't necessary for salvation, if she were to share her faith decision publicly with others it would help to seal the decision and would help her in her spiritual walk with Christ. I suggested she talk with my pastor and then share her decision with the church congregation.

Karen responded to my suggestions with a surprising statement. "My mother told me never to make this kind of decision and never to walk down the aisle of a church to declare it because I would regret it later, but that's what I want to do," she said firmly. Karen attended Sunday services with me that evening. I am sure my pastor was tired from the revival, and his sermon was particularly dry. I thought, *After this sermon, Karen is going to change her mind.* On the first verse of the song "Softly and Tenderly, Jesus is Calling," Karen walked from the second row of pews where we were sitting to declare her decision to accept Christ into her life.

I had to fight back the tears. After everyone in the church hugged Karen or greeted her with a handshake the pastor asked me to stand next to Karen while a member of the church took a Polaroid picture of Karen and me standing together hand in hand. In addition to her decision to accept Christ, Karen wanted to become a member of Bel Air Baptist Church. I taped the picture of Karen and me in the back of the Bible my parents had given me for Christmas in 1961. I wrote below the picture: *Karen, May 24, 1964, decision for Christ.* If I thought my love for Karen was strong before, I was a goner now!

Our joy in Karen's walk of faith was soon quelled when my pastor called to tell Karen's parents about her decision for Christ and her desire to join our church. After her parents considered the request they called my pastor and sternly informed him that Karen could not join our church and could no longer attend but that they would all start going to the community church a few blocks from their home. Karen and her family attended the church the next Sunday. To my knowledge that was the only time they attended while we dated. Karen's parents were not impressed with her faith decision and were unhappy with me. Her mother, who had always been cordial, told me in a rather cool manner that Karen's decision was made on the rebound after her disappointment of not making the cheerleading squad.

"Karen was vulnerable and fragile when she made the decision, but she'll get over all this," her mother declared.

I felt that Karen's mother was determined to validate her earlier warning to her daughter not to make a public commitment of faith. I wondered what had brought her to this conclusion.

Although I was disappointed and Karen was angry at her parents for their decision, our relationship grew stronger. However, the more Karen and I saw of each other, the more obstacles her parents threw in our path. Maybe her parents mistook me for a religious fanatic. If so, I understand their concerns.

As the summer approached, the intense pressure Karen's parents were putting on our relationship caused her to rebel against their authority, and they responded swiftly and decisively.

One Saturday my brother Bill and his girlfriend accompanied Karen and me on an all day outing to Lake Kanopolis, one of the few recreational lakes in Kansas. Karen's parents had given her strict orders to be back by 5 p.m. We were having a great time, and we all wanted to stay beyond Karen's curfew. We went to a nearby pay phone where Karen called to receive permission to stay out later. She returned and said with a shy smile "Everything's OK. I can stay." I then called my mom and informed her we would be late.

When we returned at 8:00 that evening Karen's parents were standing in the driveway of her home with hands on hips glaring at us. I quickly learned that Karen's parents weren't home when she called and Karen had not received permission to stay out later. Karen's parents had called my mother when we were more than an hour late.

Her mother and father scolded Karen in my presence. I was embarrassed and surprised that Karen had disobeyed her parents and therefore further compromised my relationship with them. Karen was immediately grounded and forbidden to see me for two weeks. It was an agonizing 14 days for both of us. We did talk with each other on the phone, but our calls were limited to 15 minutes a day, which seemed cruelly short.

Karen's grounding came only a few weeks into my first summer of working at Morrison Grain Elevator. The tall white concrete bins of the elevator towering over the Kansas plains were only a mile behind Karen's home. She and I had a common interest in Morrison Grain Company because her father was an executive with the company. He bought and sold grain and his office was in the Salina Board of trade where grain brokers plied their worldwide commerce.

One of my regular duties at the elevator that summer was to drive a smelly "hog truck," as we referred to it, and park it in front of the Board of Trade where I could more conveniently wheel a large dolly with a grain sack attached through the carpeted offices. I collected small bags of wheat and corn samples that had arrived to be tested before high-dollar purchase orders were issued for truckloads or train car loads of wheat and other grains. This was considered choice duty by other workers toiling in the often 100-plus-degree heat back at the elevator. Although I enjoyed the air conditioning, I was extremely uncomfortable and self-conscious in my work boots, jeans and T-shirt, which were sometimes soiled with sweat and grain dust. The male employees at the Board wore suits and ties and the female employees wore nice dresses. I stood out like a sore thumb.

We had already received complaints from some employees at the board about the foul odor of soured grain emanating from the truck that also was used to haul salvage grain to feed hogs on a Morrison-owned farm near the elevator. Before my next trip to the Board, I stopped by a car wash and used my own quarters to pay for six cycles of the hand held wand to thoroughly clean the old truck. When my boss saw the truck, he joked and said he had forgotten it was green. The next week he gave me a 20-cent-per-hour pay raise.

In spite of a more presentable truck, I was particularly uncomfortable when I had to collect the grain samples in the spacious office where Karen's father worked. He would acknowledge my presence with a quick nod of his head or brief verbal greeting.

In the weeks preceding Karen's grounding, the United States had sold millions of bushels of wheat to our then-Cold War enemy Russia to prevent starvation after several years of drought in that Communist country. The elevator manager asked me to work twelve hours a day seven days a week for the next month to empty two multimillion-bushel metal buildings filled from ground to ceiling with hard red winter wheat grown on the fertile plains of Kansas, the breadbasket of the world.

It was too hot to work in the metal buildings during the daytime heat so another employee and I worked from 7 p.m. to 7 a.m. We took turns driving a big yellow front loader tractor called a pay loader. We scooped up the wheat and dumped it into a large hopper where it was augered underground to the main grain elevator and then weighed and loaded on train cars for its eventual transport to Russia via ship. This sale of U.S.-subsidized wheat was a boon to elevators and wheat farmers who had been storing the grain from several years of record harvests in hopes of higher prices. I was glad I could do my part to help ease the Cold War, feed hungry people and help the Kansas economy.

This new night shift assignment actually helped Karen and me endure the two weeks of her grounding. Each evening when I went to work, I knew Karen was nearby even if we couldn't be together. Karen had a brilliant idea. We would write each other multi-page letters that would bypass the fetters of 15-minute phone calls and forbidden personal contact. A few minutes after 7:00 each morning I would drive up to Karen's mailbox, place my letter in the box and reach in to retrieve her letter to me. I would then turn around in her driveway and speed home so I could pore over the multiple pages of Karen's sweet words before collapsing into bed from exhaustion after continuous 12-hour work days.

Karen's parents were equally clever, and our newfound freedom of communication was soon brought to a screeching halt. In the middle of the second week of our ingenious plan, my boss and fellow church member met me a few minutes after 7 a.m. at the front gate as I was leaving work. He informed me that Karen's father had called him the day before and told him I was disturbing the neighbors with my early morning mail delivery and that I was to cease and desist. The letters Karen and I had so lovingly written to each other for delivery that morning had to wait until her grounding sentence had ended. My boss at the elevator was a good man who had chosen me for the 84-hour weeks including

the 44 hours of weekly overtime that greatly assisted in financing
my first year of college. I could see the pain in his eyes
as he calmly and dutifully delivered the message. As
the manager of the multimillion-dollar elevator and a company executive in his
own right, I'm sure he was not pleased
with the big stick his fellow executive
had asked him to wield against an 18-
year-old boy who was head over heels
in love. I was embarrassed that my
boss was given this duty and was disappointed that Karen's father did
not deliver the message himself.

In spite of the tight rein
Karen's parents kept on our relationship, we made it through the
summer. We had many wonderful and
happy experiences together, and I
dreaded leaving Karen to go off to
Kansas State University. I loved Karen, and I
often dreamed of how wonderful it would be to
marry her when I graduated from college.
However, I think we both knew how hard it
would be for our relationship to survive the pressure from her
parents and the four semesters of separation as Karen finished
high school and I continued to pursue my dream of a college degree in journalism.

I spent many moments at K-State admiring the sepia-tone
portrait of Karen that I kept on the desk in my dorm room and
wishing she was at college with me. As the weeks passed and we
settled into our separate routines, the phone calls and letters became fewer and farther apart. We had several more dates after I
left for college, but I felt as though this wonderful girl was slip-
ping away from me.

I began to hear disturbing reports about Karen from my two
brothers who still attended Salina High. Karen's circle of friends

had changed, and when I kissed her during our last few dates, the rumors that she had started smoking—something she swore never to do—were quickly confirmed. My heart ached. I continually asked God to care for Karen in this time of turmoil and rebellion in her life. Karen's parents were finally succeeding in breaking up the relationship with the college boy who seemed to pose such a threat to their daughter's well-being.

After several failed attempts to have another date with Karen, she finally agreed to go out to dinner and to a movie with me on my next weekend in Salina. I was excited about this long-awaited date, but soon after I picked her up I discovered Karen had changed. Gone were her sweet smile and her loving affection toward me. She was friendly and polite during our meal at the Wyman Motel Cafe, but she was also aloof. She talked about the growing problems with her parents and about her new circle of friends. As we entered my car for the drive to the movie, Karen dropped the bomb. "Tim, I'm sorry, but I'm tired and I don't feel like going to the movie tonight. I also have a test next week, and some of my girlfriends are coming to my house to study with me tonight. Maybe we can go to a movie another time," she added.

I was angry and hurt. I don't recall if I said a single word all the way back to Karen's house. I had made a special trip home to Salina for this date and had taken extra assignments the week before as a photographer on the *K-State Collegian* student newspaper to pay for the meal, the gasoline and the movie. However, it was far more than that. I knew our relationship had been deteriorating, and now it was over. I hated how Karen chose to tell me, but her method was effective. I didn't walk Karen to her door as I always had before. I bid her a cool goodbye, and as she got out of my car and walked toward her front door, I proceeded to squeal my tires on her smooth concrete drive as I backed out for the last time and sped away into the darkness.

My anger at Karen and at her parents temporarily masked the deep pain and loss that lurked underneath in the depths of my soul. I hated the sense of loss and betrayal that followed such wonderful times with Karen. My stomach was again in knots after the loss of a second steady girlfriend in a little more than a year. I could no longer contain my emotions. I cursed and the tears gushed down my cheeks as I drove home to the refuge of my supportive family. Maybe Karen's parents were right. Maybe her infatuation with me and her faith commitment were merely temporary soothing ointments on the wound left from failing to be rechosen as a cheerleader. Maybe I had misjudged Karen's feelings toward me as often happens in teenage relationships. Maybe the pressure of parents and friends was too much for this impressionable teenager to handle. We all have our breaking points. In the months that followed I unfortunately allowed my concern for and thoughts of Karen to dominate my first semester of college to the great detriment of my academics.

Throughout my life I have continued to pray for the well-being of the first two loves in my life—Cheryl and Karen. I learned much from both of them. I owe much to both of them. They helped to teach me both the joy and the disappointments that life can bring. They left their enriching indelible ink on my life, which I believe made me a better husband to the woman who finally brought true and enduring love and friendship into my life. The ups and downs of these early love relationships also helped me to be a better father to three beautiful daughters and two lovely granddaughters who all continue to enrich my life daily.

I saw Karen only one time after I left the two black tire marks on her driveway. I am sorry for my childish exit from her life. Karen was working in a Salina grocery store a year after our breakup when I saw her for the last time. I don't know if she saw me or not. Over the years as each of my three daughters turned 16, I realized anew that Karen and I were only children when I thought we were so much in love.

Five years later and shortly after my wife Linda and I were married, my brother Steve handed me a copy of the society section of the *Kansas City Star*. It contained the engagement announcement of Karen and her fiancé. "How does that make you feel?" Steve asked. "Are you sad?"

"No," I replied.

I was happy and at peace for Karen. If my prayers were answered Karen had outgrown her rebellion and had found a wonderful lifelong mate.

As I look back as a 57-year-old grandfather, I do hope Karen has some fond memories of our time together. I hope she has never regretted the day she asked Christ to come into her life. I hope she has never regretted making a public declaration of her commitment to Christ. I hope she made peace with her parents. I believe they wanted only the best for their youngest daughter.

At the end of my first semester in college, my mother helped me deal with the second lost romance of my life. After a reassuring talk with my mom, I removed the picture of Karen and me from the back of my Bible. It brought closure to a wonderful but bittersweet relationship.

At 1 a.m. on February 22, 2002, in the middle of writing this entry for my book, I opened the Bible my parents had given me for Christmas in 1961. The yellow stains from where the tape held the picture of Karen and me in place are still there along with several scripture verses that I recorded during our six months of challenging courtship that flew by so swiftly.

Underneath the empty space where the picture used to be are the words printed by me in indelible blue ink 38 years ago: "Karen, May 24, 1964, decision for Christ." Today I have the assurance that Karen is still where I left her nearly four decades ago—in the hollow of God's hand.

Entry 15

Trader Tim

1966—Salina, Kansas

In 1966 on a Christmas break from my sophomore year at Kansas State University, I decided my 1962 Ford station wagon with 160,000 miles was on its last leg. It had served my family and me well. My father had sold it to me and financed it for me after it had successfully hauled newspapers seven days a week for three years. The odometer now showed only 60,000 of the 160,000 hard in-town miles. In those days the odometer rolled back to zero as it passed 100,000 miles because in most cases cars didn't last much longer than that.

I was 19 that Christmas, and I already was driving my third car and second motorcycle. I was 15 when my brother Steve sold me my first car, a 1952 customized Plymouth coup. The Plymouth would rarely start when the temperature dipped below freezing, which is quite often during Kansas winters. My second vehicle was an equally worn-out 1960 Ford station wagon that my dad had used as a newspaper delivery vehicle. I, too, used it to help my dad throw newspapers seven days a week.

The acquisition of my two motorcycles seemed like a gift. I worked 20 hours a week as a photographer and reporter for the *Manhattan Daily Mercury* newspaper to pay my way through college. The local Honda motorcycle dealer in Manhattan, Kansas, enlisted my talents as a newspaper photographer to shoot 24 pictures for ads of college students riding Hondas in all kinds of locations throughout Manhattan and on campus. The ads ran in *The K-State Collegian* student newspaper under the slogan "You meet the nicest people on a Honda." The first 12 ads were photographed in trade for a shiny black Honda S-65 motorcycle. My fee on the next 12 ads was higher, and I received a larger and sleeker black and silver Honda S-90 motorcycle that I could carry back and forth from college in a rack on the back of my station wagon.

I promptly sold the S-65 Honda to my brother Phil, who was only 14 but who rode it to throw papers every day for nearly a year until a police officer pulled him over and issued him a ticket with a hefty fine for driving without a permit. Fortunately he only had to stable his mechanical steed a few months until his 15th birthday, when he received his learner's permit and became a legitimate driver.

Several of my buddies and I rode our motorcycles all around Manhattan, often late at night, when we should have been studying. The S-65 and S-90, which now seem little larger than bicycles beside today's powerful motorcycles, were true freedom machines.

As a veteran vehicle owner with three used cars and two new motorcycles to my credit I was ready to move up to a better car. The faint knocking in the motor of the Ford after a trip home from college on the interstate was a foreboding sound.

The Volkswagen beetle, popular in those days with the hippie generation (whose lifestyle I never emulated), was considered to be a fuel-efficient, solidly built piece of German workmanship that would provide many years of performance. Some of the VW beetle's characteristics flew in the face of American automobile manufacturing and culture. American carmakers showcased new body styles nearly every year to attract new customers into the showroom. Volkswagen concentrated on improving the mechanics and reliability of the German-made beetle each year with little or no changes to the basic body style. Everything on the car was included in the base purchase price. The rear-engine, air-cooled rear-wheel drive configuration also was in vast contrast to American-made vehicles. This penchant for well-built automobiles and my penchant for driving something different and state-of-the-art attracted me to the VW showroom.

In those days VW dealerships were rather elitist. The salesmen acted as if they were doing you a favor if they sold you a VW. Most cities were allowed only one VW dealership and no local competition. The only negotiating was the allowance made for your trade-in if you had one. Bargaining for a discount on a VW was considered verboten (forbidden) and low class! I'll never forget the tall, distinguished salesman who greeted me at the door of the VW dealership. He was formal and probably doubted my financial ability to purchase a car. However, after a few minutes of sharing my engineering knowledge of his elite beetle, his friendly Kansas underpinnings emerged from behind the wall of sophistication the German marketing manuals had built for this salesman.

I told him my intention was to buy the black VW beetle on the showroom floor and to return with my father who would cosign the loan for the difference between my Ford station wagon and this precision German machine. I'm sure he didn't expect to see this poor college student again.

I drove home barely able to contain myself and laid out my plans before my father.

"Son, you don't want some foreign-made car," my dad said. "That car's too small, and besides, you can't afford a new car and college tuition, too. What's wrong with the one you have, Tim? No, I won't cosign the loan!" my father declared with finality.

A few minutes later I was on the phone with my brother Steve, who was 23 years old and had a lucrative job as an apprentice pressman with the *Wichita Eagle Newspaper* in Wichita, Kansas, 90 miles away.

My father had also refused to cosign for Steve on a 1954 Corvette when Steve was 19. Ironically, that same car today is worth anywhere from $60,000 to $100,000—more than my father made in 10 years of hard employment. Steve had no older brother to turn to and passed up "the deal of a lifetime."

Steve, who by now had purchased multiple cars and motorcycles himself, wasted no time in driving to Salina to defy both the elitism of the VW dealer and my father's refusal to cosign my loan.

The next day Steve and I prepared my tired Ford wagon for the "deal making." The morning of the trade we thoroughly cleaned the interior and exterior of the car and waxed the paint to a high shine. With three pints of motor honey in the crankcase the knocking in the engine had completely vanished.

The blue cloth front seat in the otherwise brown interior of the '62 Ford wagon should have been a dead giveaway to the VW dealer. The first seat had been worn out from my father's heavy frame and the constant sliding of newspapers across the front seat. Steve and I had gone to a junkyard a few months earlier and found a replacement seat from a wrecked car with blue interior. As we headed for the VW dealer we knew the $1,700 sticker price on the 1967 VW bug on the showroom floor was non-negotiable, but Steve and I were undaunted. We were hoping to get at least $200 out of the old Ford. She was looking her best that day.

We paced the parking lot and the showroom impatiently as the VW salesman who was part-owner of the dealership took the Ford for a test drive. When he returned he walked slowly around the car looking at every imperfection.

We held our breath as he raised the hood to examine the newly washed engine that belied its true condition. The salesman listened intently as he revved the engine from the accelerator linkage on the carburetor. He closed the hood, turned off the engine and said, "Come on in, boys. Let me sell you the finest car available in

America." My heart was pounding as we sat down at the negotiating table. What if he failed to offer the $200 I needed to swing the deal?

"She seems to have a lot of wear on her, but you've cleaned her up real nice," the salesman said. "The engine sounds good, too. However, with that non-matching seat cover, I'm afraid all I can allow you is $500," he stated firmly.

There was a long silence as I regained my composure. I couldn't believe my ears. "So that's $1,200 difference plus tax—right?" I asked.

"Yes, that's right," the dealer responded,

Steve and I looked at each other, trying to keep straight faces. "Well, I don't know," I replied, "I was hoping for a little more." At that moment Steve started kicking me under the table. I guess he thought I was going to blow the deal.

"Mr. Fields, I'd like for you to take this VW home with you, and that's a generous offer," he countered.

"Well, I guess I'll take your offer then," I said with a slight tone of dejection. Steve stopped kicking me and started poking my side instead in congratulations. After shaking the salesman's hand to seal the deal, we walked behind him to to view our new purchase and smiled broadly at each other to mark our accomplishment.

Steve and I laughed all the way home. We had received more than twice as much as we expected to get out of the tired old Ford. We were triumphant.

As we pulled into the driveway of our home, my father greeted us with a frown and a puzzled expression. "What have you boys done?" he queried as he shook his head back and forth in disapproval. My father's reaction was especially sweet for Steve who, with this aggressive move felt as though he had rightfully taken his place as head of the family and had deposed the power of my father, who had driven him from home at age 17 to face the world on his own.

This was not to be the last car loan my brother and fellow car lover Steve would cosign for me. We experienced many more deal-making adventures in the following decades. An even greater affirmation of our VW deal making came on my next visit to the VW dealership for the first scheduled oil change.

The car salesman saw me drive in and wasted no time in asking me how I liked the new car. "Son, I have been selling cars for 25 years, and this is the first time anyone, especially a teenager, has bested me in a car trade. We had to sell that Ford to a farmer to haul hay to feed his cows," the salesman said with a wince. "That car was worn out, and the engine started knocking a few days after you traded it," he said. "You're a good car trader, son! We lost money on that deal!"

Before my Christmas vacation was over, the little rear-engine VW won over my skeptical father. After an unusually fierce blizzard with drifts of snow in the streets several feet deep my father's 1964 Ford Fairmont station wagon couldn't make it through the snow to deliver newspapers to our carriers and newspaper racks.

"Come on, Dad," I said. "I'll show you what a real car will do." With the weight of the rear-mounted engine over the drive wheels and the back seat of the VW bug loaded to the ceiling with newspapers, the little car bit through the snow, sometimes almost sledding over it. At the end of our newspaper delivery route, my father admitted, "Well, I guess this little car is good for something after all, son. I'm impressed."

Lest anyone should feel sorry for the VW dealer, the same salesman was shocked and pleased when I came in a year later to buy a new 1968 VW light blue fastback coupe after I sold my 1967 VW to my brother Bill. Without a trade, he discounted the more expensive 1968 VW $200 and threw in a set of floor mats (an unheard-of discount at a VW dealer). He seemed to respect my persistent negotiating and repeat business.

Over the years I have bought, sold and traded cars many times. While employed at the Baptist Brotherhood Commission in Memphis, two of the editors wrote stories of my car-buying "habit" and how I had represented them and scores of others in negotiating with car dealers in pursuit of a fair deal. Everywhere I went, people were asking me to help them sell their old car or go with them to the dealer to buy a new one.

Fellow editors Charlie Warren and Larry Jerden each wrote about me in one of their weekly columns in *The World Missions Journal.*

One article was entitled "Trader Tim." Warren called my car antics "a ministry" and told how he had driven the Pontiac station wagon I had sold him with 30,000 miles on it for five trouble-free years. Many years later he told me he still owned the car and it was running strong. What I didn't admit to Charlie was that I secretly admired his frugality and wished that I had such good sense.

As I write this entry it is 6:30 a.m. on Saturday, September 14, 2002, and two days ago I purchased my 44th Honda from the Trickett Honda dealership in Nashville, Tennessee, with the help of veteran sales representative Barbara Moore. Barbara sold me the first Honda in 1980 shortly after I moved to Nashville. I already had purchased six Hondas and 15 Pontiacs and other assorted General Motors cars from a dealer in Memphis. I have referred hundreds of car-buying friends to Barbara over the years and some are on their fourth or fifth Honda. Reed Trickett, whose family owns the dealership, even recruited me for several radio and television commercials promoting the dealership.

I have personally owned more than 140 cars and 8 motorcycles in 41 years of vehicle buying. That's an average of more than three vehicle purchases a year. After all these years I have stopped counting vehicles. When my three daughters were in high school and college I had the joy of keeping five cars at our home at all times. Much of the time we had five Hondas. I was in car-buying heaven.

I have literally helped hundreds of people save money by locating buyers for their cars or by helping them purchase cars at dealerships or from individuals. I view it as a way of helping others in the often daunting and expensive task of car buying and negotiating. That is probably the only redeeming benefit of my addiction to the automobile. In addition, I have contributed to the income of the families of many auto workers, car manufacturers, car dealerships, car salespeople, banks, insurance companies and auto accessory stores. Just think what all this car buying and selling has contributed to the American economy!

The 50th Honda sitting in my garage is a sleek silver 2003 Honda Accord EX four-door sedan. The new Honda takes its place beside a maroon 2002 Honda CRV that my wife drives and my 2002 bright red Honda Interceptor sport motorcycle.

In almost every case when I have traded one car for another I inevitably have buyer's remorse. This trade is no exception. It is the remorse of a renewal of perpetual payments or the fact that the car I traded in still smelled new. My remorse is probably akin to an alcoholic who goes on a drinking binge and tears up the joint. When he awakens from his stupor, he is remorseful that once again he has succumbed to the lure of the bottle and the reality that his failure to resist temptation has resulted in a hefty bill for damages.

Many car purchases ago I proclaimed myself a true "caraholic"— unable to resist the siren song of a new model in my love affair with the automobile! Only my "deal making" has made the ongoing ordeal financially survivable. I am now on a three-year cycle with my Hondas. However, I have purchased five motorcycles in the last five years and have assisted my daughters and sons-in-law in their purchase of several more automobiles during that time.

This love affair with vehicles (both two-wheel and four-wheel) like the love I have for my wife, daughters, granddaughters, sons-in-law and other family members, has brought me much pleasure and sometimes pain. The pleasure of having owned and driven nearly 150 different automobiles and motorcycles is evident to any other vehicle connoisseur. The pain comes from knowing I could now be retired if I had invested the money spent on sales tax, down payments, loan interest and loan payments!

My wife Linda was forewarned about my addiction by my college pastor Fred Hollomon before we were married. When we both went to him for premarital counseling, he said "Linda, there is just one thing I need to warn you about with Tim. He has a problem with motorcycles and cars."

"Oh that's alright," she replied. "I'll solve that."

"You don't understand, Linda," he said forcefully. "He has a serious problem. He has had two motorcycles and five cars in only four years of college. I've only had three cars in my whole life," pastor Hollomon exclaimed.

Over the years Linda has tolerated my addiction to vehicles, although I know it pains her and me as well. I guess she knew she was fighting a losing battle. Only once did I take back a car, telling the salesperson my marriage might fail if I kept it.

Many times I have asked God to forgive me of this addiction to cars and often I have prayed for the strength to resist another purchase. Linda has said she's going to bury me in a car with my hands strapped to the wheel. What a way to go!

During a break in writing this entry I told Linda, "These two Honda automobiles in our garage are keepers. We'll have them until we retire."

Linda turned to look at me and simply smiled.

Entry 16

True Love

1968–69—Kansas City, Missouri; Memphis, Tennessee; Manhattan, Kansas

By the end of my freshman year in college at Kansas State University, I had overcome the disappointment of my dissolved romance with Karen, my second high school sweetheart.

My first year at K-State, I worked as a photographer for the *K-State Collegian*. I was paid $2 per photo. In my sophomore and succeeding years at K-State I worked as a photographer and reporter for the daily *Manhattan Mercury*. As a photographer I had a sideline pass to every K-State sporting event including football, basketball, track, tennis and wrestling.

I dated several girls during my college days, but none measured up to my first two romances of high school days. I was shy and often too afraid to ask girls out for fear of being turned down. I often wished a girl could do the asking if she liked a guy. In order to improve my odds of getting the right girl I decided to get my crooked teeth fixed. During the early summer between my junior and senior years I visited an orthodontist in Salina, Kansas, and started wearing braces, which my parents could never afford. My orthodontist put me on a weekly payment plan, and I was one of only a few college students wearing the uncomfortable and unsightly appliances. Most kids had their braces off before entering high school.

Later that summer the Vietnam War was raging. I, along with about 60 other guys, were summoned by the draft board to take a bus from Salina to Kansas City, Missouri, to report for possible induction into the army. Like every other guy on the bus, I was fearful. I wanted to finish college, and my stint in the Air Force ROTC program as a college freshman taught me enough to know I preferred to go in as an officer, not as a private inductee. However, it was too late now for that.

I thought of every possible way I could put off going to war. I wanted to serve my country, but on better terms. During my junior year in college, I had experienced several bouts of severe muscle trauma in my lower back. At one point I couldn't get out of bed for several days. My brother Bill and three dorm mates had carried me to my car and then into the student health clinic, where I was given muscle relaxants and hot pack treatments to get me back on my feet again.

Prior to my bus ride to Kansas City I had secured a note from my doctor verifying these debilitating bouts with lower back pain. I hoped the doctor's notes would be enough to delay my induction until I graduated from college.

My bus mates and I filed into the induction center for our physicals, frightened about our future. I passed all of the tests with flying colors, but because of my medical note I was sent to a doctor's station where my case was reviewed.

"So, Mr. Fields, you're a college student. Is that correct?" he asked.

"Yes sir," I replied.

"Mr. Fields, according to the physical exam we gave you and the nature of this note, I don't see your back problems keeping you from military service. Your back can be strengthened through exercise."

With those words my heart sank. "Now, Mr. Fields, my notes show you are wearing orthodontic braces. Let me see them," he requested. I smiled broadly to expose the mass of metal wires and bands.

"Do you think you can graduate in a year?" the doctor asked.

"Yes sir, I'll be a senior next year," I replied.

"You can't get those braces adjusted every month on the field of combat," he asserted. "I'm going to reclassify you from 1-A to 4-F. That makes you ineligible for military service for medical reasons for the next 12 months," he explained. "You go back to school this fall and get that college degree," he urged. "Get back on that bus and go home," he instructed.

"Yes sir, I will," I stammered as I shook his outstretched hand.

Only a handful of my bus mates returned to Salina that day. The rest stayed in Kansas City to be inducted into the army.

I returned home with a great sense of relief and disbelief. I felt as if I had been rescued from the jaws of hell. I also had lingering feelings of guilt when I thought about the young men who would soon be fighting and maybe dying for our country. That relief and guilt grew when several months later in the national draft lottery my birthday was not drawn until number 354. Men were drafted in the order their birthday was drawn starting with number 1. Draft quotas at that time were being fulfilled in the high 200s. My chances of being drafted with number 354 were almost nil.

I have often wondered how many of my bus mates from Salina never made it back home from Vietnam. I owe all Vietnam veterans, both living and dead, a debt I can never repay.

At the beginning of my senior year I felt God calling me to a career in religious journalism. I dreamed of working for *Decision* magazine published by the Billy Graham organization or working for my own Baptist denomination in communications. I even shared my intention for full-time Christian service with my pastor and then our entire congregation one Sunday morning.

During this same time period I met Susan and Sharon (not their real names), beautiful blond-haired identical twin sisters. Susan was dating one of the residence assistants in the dorm where I lived. He introduced me to Sharon. I dated Sharon throughout my senior year at K-State. She was quiet, shy and reserved. She and her sister were from a small farming community in western Kansas.

Sharon was a head turner. She and her sister were always well-dressed and well-accessorized and their makeup was well-applied. I often felt self-conscious when other guys looked at Sharon while I was with her.

Sharon often accompanied me on Friday nights on photographic assignments for *The Manhattan Mercury*. I took pictures of area high school basketball or football games. Sometimes we would go to three games in one night, staying at each game only long enough to get a good action photo for Sunday's paper. After the games, Sharon and I would eat a late supper or go to a 9 p.m. movie. Sharon rarely turned down an opportunity to be with me, and we often rode around Manhattan on my motorcycle. I began to think of her as a potential mate.

As the months passed, we continued dating, but our relationship lacked the emotional closeness for which I yearned. Sharon occasionally attended my small Southern Baptist church with me or went to social events with other college students from my church, but she did not seem to share my enthusiasm for matters of faith.

After I started dating Sharon I explored the possibility of attending seminary and earning a master's degree in religious education. Sharon never said much when I shared this idea with her. I had an uneasy feeling that our year-long relationship was not growing as I had hoped.

Some of my dates with Sharon were interrupted by opportunities to photograph and write about events that would be published in the next day's edition of the *Manhattan Mercury*. Working for the newspaper was one of the highlights of my college years. As I finished classes each day I would call the newspaper on my CB radio and get my photo assignments. I had a police monitor in my car and often raced to a fire or serious automobile wreck whenever I heard the call.

I needed more money to pay for college loans and ongoing college expenses, so I increasingly worked more hours for the newspaper as both photographer and reporter and spent less effort on my class work. Working in my profession may have prepared me better for my career than my college courses in journalism.

During my senior year I dropped one course the first semester and one the second semester. Near the end of my senior year in chemistry class, I had a "C" in lab and an "F" in lecture, which averaged out to a "D" for the course. I went to see my lecture professor to find out my final grade before leaving for the summer.

He checked my final lecture paper, which showed a "D." However, while I was standing there he found an error my lab teacher had made when grading my paper. Correcting the error cost me two points, and my "D" became an "F." If I hadn't been so impatient I would have passed chemistry and had four more hours of credit. As a result, I was now 10 hours short of graduating. This terrible setback prompted me to reassess my life and refocus on academics.

I had already been accepted for entrance as a religious education student at Midwestern Baptist Theological Seminary in Kansas City, Missouri, for the fall 1968 term with the understanding that I would finish my undergraduate coursework by the fall of 1969.

For the summer I returned to Salina, where I enrolled in six hours of literature at Marymount College and painted houses for income. I enjoyed my classes, which included six students who were Catholic nuns and eight other women. The professor also was a nun. Those courses provided many opportunities for an exchange of religious ideas and broadened the horizons and broke stereotypes for the nuns and for me as a future Baptist seminarian. The six hours of "A" on my grade report for the summer lifted my spirits and raised my college grade point average.

Midwestern allowed me to start seminary with the agreement that I would finish my bachelor of science in journalism the next summer. The seminary also hired me as news director. I was excited about the seminary and about my new job and also because my brother Steve would be starting medical school in Kansas City that same semester.

For financial reasons Sharon and her twin sister had dropped out of school for a semester but stayed on in Manhattan, where they both worked for a bookstore on the edge of the K-State campus. Sharon and I each occasionally had dates with other people during this time but continued to communicate by phone and letter. We dated whenever I could make the trip from Kansas City to Manhattan. My desire to find a wife was growing, and I felt my best chances of finding the right mate had eluded me while I was in college.

I was determined to strengthen my relationship with Sharon or find someone else. On a visit to Manhattan in November, Susan's boyfriend, who was still a residence assistant at K-State, told me he knew a silversmith and was planning to order a custom-made sterling silver ring for Susan for Christmas. "Would you like to order a matching one for Sharon?" he asked. "Since they are twins, that would be pretty cool." I agreed and gave him the money.

That same weekend Sharon asked if I would like to meet her parents and said she might invite me to her hometown sometime after Christmas. A few weeks later the ring arrived in the mail. It was simple but unique. I looked forward to giving it to Sharon.

During this time my brother Steve was dating a girl he had met while attending Oklahoma Baptist University in Shawnee, Oklahoma. Judy was now a Navy nurse stationed at the Naval Air Station in Memphis. Her roommate was a Navy nurse from Bartlesville, Oklahoma.

A week before Christmas Steve called and said, "Tim, Judy and I want to fix you up on a date with her roommate Linda Walls. We'll leave in my Corvette the day after Christmas and you'll have a date with Linda that night. Alright?" he asked.

"I don't know, I might be going to western Kansas to see Sharon then," I replied.

"No, you and I are going to Memphis," Steve said firmly.

"Well, what does she look like?" I asked.

"What difference does it make?" he replied. "She graduated magna cum laude and was named the outstanding senior nursing student at the University of Oklahoma. She has two sisters and six brothers, so she grew up poor like we did. Her father has a Ph.D. from Princeton and her mother went to nursing school, too. Linda's a Baptist and she's cute. You'll like her." he assured. "Get your bags packed. It's a done deal," he barked and then hung up the phone.

My head was spinning. *What have I agreed to do?* I wondered. At 5 a.m. on December 26, 1968, Steve and I left in his silver 1968

Corvette for the 550-mile trip to Memphis. I can't say what our top speed was, but we made it in less than 8 hours. Linda was on duty at the hospital for the 7 a.m. to 3 p.m. shift, so Judy drove us to the Naval Hospital. We met Linda in the halls of the sick oficers quarters where she was charge nurse that day. Linda was dressed in her Navy nursing uniform, which was white from head to toe except for the black stripes and gold braid on her nurse's cap that signified her rank as a lieutenant. Her beauiful brown eyes, attractive figure and engaging smile captured my attention.

We nervously greeted one another and agreed to meet at her house a few hours later for our double date with Judy and Steve. That night we went out to eat and then to a movie with Steve and Judy. After the movie Linda and I shared our life stories. The next day Steve and Judy went their way, and Linda and I went ours. Linda took me on a tour of the Naval base and of Memphis. That night, after another meal with Judy and Steve, we went in two cars to the banks of the Mississippi River. The night air was cold and the sky was clear. The moon and stars shone brightly as we sat in separate cars with our dates. Linda and I held hands and shared our life dreams and our faith journeys as we watched the tug boats with their heavy laden barges churn their way down the Mississippi River. Like the current of the mighty river, our dreams and aspirations seemed to be flowing in the same direction.

We hugged and kissed and talked past midnight. A sudden wave of enlightenment engulfed me in the realization that in 24 hours I had shared more with this girl and knew more about her family, dreams, goals and personal faith than I had shared or knew about Sharon after nearly 18 months of dating.

For some reason, when I left Kansas City I brought with me the custom-made sterling silver ring I had ordered for Sharon's Christmas present. I reached in my coat pocket and retrieved the ring, which was nestled in cotton in a small silver foil-covered box. I thanked Linda for the wonderful time we had together and placed the box in her hand. "This is my late Christmas present to you," I said. Linda opened the box and was shocked to see the ring. I placed it on her finger and it fit.

"How did you know what size I wore?" she asked.

"I was just lucky," I answered.

Steve and I returned to Kansas City the next day but I couldn't get Linda out of my mind. We were closely in sync in our family upbringing, our faith in Christ and our goals in life. She was attractive, extremely intelligent and down-to-earth. We talked about all aspects of our lives. However, I was not immediately smitten with her and she felt the same about me.

In the following weeks I called Linda several times. In an offhand comment she said, "Tim, you should fly to Memphis one weekend and see me."

"I'd love to. I've never flown in my life," I replied, "but I can't afford a plane ticket."

"If you'll come I'll pay for your airfare," Linda offered.

"Are you serious?" I asked.

"Sure, just make the reservation for next weekend and I'll send you the money," she said.

"OK, I'll take you up on that," I agreed.

The next evening Linda called and said, "Tim, I have been thinking about my offer to fly you to Memphis, and I've changed my mind. I don't think that would be a good idea," she said.

"Well, I'm sorry Linda, I've already made the reservation and I'm coming anyway," I said resolutely.

There was a long pause and then Linda said, "OK, I guess it will be alright."

In the next five months Linda and I talked on the phone almost daily. Steve's romance with Judy grew steadily, and we made many whirlwind trips in his Corvette to visit the Navy nurses. Judy and Linda flew to see us whenever they could.

Ironically, Sharon never called to ask me to come to western Kansas to meet her parents. I know Susan knew about the ring I had ordered for Sharon because I asked Susan for Sharon's ring size. Sharon and I exchanged a few letters after my first few dates with Linda, but our relationship was all but over.

In the months that followed, Linda and I grew closer, and the flames of love were kindled. We talked openly about each other's desires and expectations for a marriage partner. After much prayer and reflection I believed some day I would ask Linda to marry me.

In June I attended summer school at Kansas State University to finish my journalism degree. One afternoon I saw Sharon and Susan walking from work to their home. I gave them a ride home and exchanged pleasantries.

They invited me to have supper at a local restaurant with them that night, and I met them there. We talked about school and family. I was sitting next to Sharon, and she placed her hand on the top of my thigh. This was the first time she had ever been that openly affectionate. I wasn't sure what to think.

Although I was almost certain that Linda would someday be my wife, little doubts kept creeping into my mind. *What if Sharon really is the one?* I would wonder in a moment of senseless confusion. *Maybe I'll date both Linda and Sharon this summer and then I'll know for sure by fall,* I surmised. Inwardly I knew that was dishonest.

Each evening that summer, after I finished classes and my day's work as a newspaper photographer, I delivered a complimentary copy of the day's issue of the *Manhattan Mercury* to the front door of Susan and Sharon's basement apartment as I had done regularly during my senior year in college.

One day as I rounded the corner of their apartment, I was stunned to find Sharon in an intimate embrace in the arms of a strange man only a few feet in front of me.

"Oh excuse me, Sharon," I said as I dropped the newspaper at the feet of the startled couple. I then swiftly retreated to my car. It was the last newspaper I ever delivered to the twins.

A few days later I invited Linda to fly to Kansas City, where I agreed to pick her up and then show her around K-State and the *Manhattan Mercury.*

I had been open with Linda about my dating history with Sharon. My brother Phil was going to summer school, so when Linda asked about the twins, Phil quickly agreed to take her into the bookstore to observe them at the checkout desks where they were working. I was leery about this, but I agreed.

A few minutes later Linda and Phil returned with sly smiles on their faces. "So, they sure are prim and pretty Tim. Are you sure you don't like that beautiful chick more than me?" Linda queried.

"No, I'm in love with you," I said.

Linda had an evening flight out of Kansas City, and she was nervous about the possibility of missing her flight and being AWOL (absent without leave) from duty the next morning.

As we drove back to Kansas City on I-35 I continued to tease Linda, suggesting I could date both her and Sharon during the rest of summer school. I glanced across the car at Linda and noticed she was crying.

"What's the matter Linda?" I asked. "Are you upset because I'm teasing you about dating Sharon this summer?"

"No," Linda replied. "I'm OK."

I thought to myself, *How totally insensitive of me. I'm a jerk. This is the woman I want to spend the rest of my life with, and I'm playing games with her.*

Immediately I pulled my 1969 Camaro convertible to the shoulder of I-35 and took Linda's hand in mine. As cars whizzed by I said, "I'm sorry I've been teasing you, Linda. I want to ask you right now if you will be my wife. Will you marry me?" I asked expectantly.

"You don't have to ask me to marry you," she said. "I know you were just teasing about Sharon."

"What do you mean I don't have to ask you? I do have to ask you! Will you marry me?" I asked fervently.

"Yes I will," she replied as she looked into my pitiful eyes and squeezed my hand.

"Can we go now?" Linda urged. "I wasn't crying about Sharon," she explained. "I was crying because I'm afraid I'm going to miss my flight back to Memphis and be in trouble with the Navy if I do," she said.

Linda and I have laughed over the years about my proposal. The reason for her tears tells volumes about who she is. She always does what she agrees to do and more, and she performs every task to the best of her ability. It is one of the many reasons I love her so much.

A few weeks later I bought Linda an engagement ring in the post exchange at Naval Air Station Memphis. It was strange to see the enlisted men salute Linda, who was an officer, as we walked across the base.

Two months later on August 9, 1969, we were married at First Baptist Church, Bartlesville, Oklahoma, in a simple wedding attended by members of our large families. The temperature outside was 110 degrees.

The next week we spent our honeymoon going to and from Baltimore, Maryland, to the wedding of Steve and Judy, who had introduced us less than eight months earlier.

After more than 33 years of marriage and the birth and rearing of three daughters, our love for each other grows daily.

The words of my mother spoken to a heartsick boy several years earlier rang true. "God has someone special in mind for you Tim....God will help you find that girl when the time is right."

My mother's words were prophetic. God helped me to wait for and to recognize true love. I am thankful to God and to Linda for the priceless indelible ink Linda continues to write on the pages of my life!

Postscript

The publishing of *Indelible Ink: A Baby Boomer's Diary* is the fulfillment of a personal dream. I wrote it to serve multiple purposes. I wrote it as a partial family history to be passed down among succeeding generations. I wrote it to share life experiences with others and to encourage others to share their own stories. Through happy and sad times, through laughter and tears, humankind can be strengthened by sharing stories of struggle and success.

Professor Hugh Wamble at Midwestern Baptist Theological Seminary often told his students, "If you want to leave a legacy that outlives you, write a book!"

This book is my dream and a part of my legacy. If one of your dreams is to write a book, Fields Publishing stands ready to help you fulfill that dream.

Contact us at the address below and we will share with you how we can help you to turn your dream into reality. —Tim Fields

Fields Publishing Inc.
917 Harpeth Valley Place
Nashville, Tennessee 37221
Phone: 615-662-1344
E-mail: tim_fields@fieldspublishing.com
Website: www.fieldspublishing.com

About the Artist

Nancy C. Hall is an elementary school art teacher in art education and curriculum design in the Nashville, Tennessee, public schools.

Hall grew up in California and New Mexico, where she developed a love for the desert and a curiosity about tribal peoples. She traveled as a guest of the Netherlands Diplomatic Corps to Algeria. Inspired by her work there, she returned to the United States to earn a degree in art education from Vanderbilt University.

Hall then worked in the Sultanate of Oman concentrating on images of the ocean, desert, local architecture and tribal costumes.

Hall has lived in Scotland and the Netherlands, where her silkscreen prints of period architecture culminated in an exhibition sponsored by the National Trust of Scotland.

In 1998 Hall returned to the United States to rear her family. In addition to teaching, she is exploring her Native American heritage through a series of work featuring the Natchez Trace in oils, watercolors, silk-screen prints and multimedia.

In addition to *Indelible Ink,* her illustration work includes dust jacket designs for award-winning authors Karen Lowachee and James Stoddard. She also illustrated the book *Matt the Moody Hermit Crab,* the first book ever written for children with bipolar disorder.

About the Author

Timothy J. Fields was born in 1946 in Wichita, Kansas. In 1956 he moved to Salina, Kansas, with his parents and four brothers. Fields earned a Bachelor of Science in journalism from Kansas State University and a Master of Religious Education degree from Midwestern Baptist Theological Seminary.

During college and seminary he worked as a reporter and photographer for the *Daily K-State Collegian* and the *Manhattan Daily Mercury*. He was a photographer and reporter during a summer internship for the *Salina Journal*. Fields also served as news director for Midwestern Seminary and then for two years as reporter and photographer for the *North Kansas City Dispatch* and *Platte County Dispatch* (Townsend) newspapers while in seminary.

Fields married Navy nurse Linda Walls in 1969, and in 1971 they moved to Memphis, Tennessee, where he was a magazine and products editor for the Southern Baptist Brotherhood Commission. Linda was a staff nurse and later director of nursing for Saint Jude Children's Research Hospital. In 1980 Tim and Linda and their three daughters moved to Nashville, Tennessee, where Tim became director of communications and then vice president for product development for the Southern Baptist Christian Life Commission. In 1988 he became associate executive director of the Southern Baptist Education Commission. That same year he established Fields Publishing Inc.

Since 1996 Fields has worked for the Association of Southern Baptist Colleges and Schools as director of communications and managing editor of the *Southern Baptist Educator*. He also serves as president of Fields Publishing, which publishes books for churches, individuals and other organizations. Fields is a member of Immanuel Baptist Church, where his wife is church administrator. He teaches a senior men's Sunday School class and is an ordained deacon. In addition to their three daughters, Tim and Linda have two granddaughters.